# The Importance of Being Innocent
## Why we worry about children

**Joanne Faulkner** is an Australian Research Council (ARC) post-doctoral fellow in the School of History and Philosophy at the University of New South Wales.

Other titles in the *Australian Encounters* series
(Series editor: Tony Moore)

Tim Soutphommasane
*Reclaiming Patriotism: Nation-building for Australian progressives*

Milissa Deitz
*Watch this Space: The future of Australian journalism*

Rodney Cavalier
*Power Crisis: The self-destruction of a state Labor Party*

# The Importance of Being Innocent
## Why we worry about children

Joanne Faulkner

MONASH University

CAMBRIDGE
UNIVERSITY PRESS

NATIONAL
CENTRE FOR
AUSTRALIAN
STUDIES

CAMBRIDGE UNIVERSITY PRESS
Cambridge, New York, Melbourne, Madrid, Cape Town, Singapore,
São Paulo, Delhi, Dubai, Tokyo, Mexico City

Cambridge University Press
477 Williamstown Road, Port Melbourne, VIC 3207, Australia

Published in the United States of America by Cambridge University Press, New York

www.cambridge.org
Information on this title: www.cambridge.org/9780521146975

First published 2011

Designed by Adrian Saunders
Typeset by Aptara Corp.
Printed in Australia by Ligare Pty Ltd

*A catalogue record for this publication is available from the British Library*

*National Library of Australia Cataloguing in Publication data*
    Faulkner, Joanne.
    The importance of being innocent: why we worry about children / Joanne Faulkner.
    9780521146975 (pbk.)
    Australian encounters.
    Includes index.
    Children – Australia.
    Children in advertising – Australia.
    Sex in advertising – Australia.
    Advertising – Psychological aspects.
    Child molesters – Australia.
    Pedophilia – Australia.
362.760994

ISBN 978-0-521-14697-5 Paperback

# Contents

# Acknowledgements

An earlier version of some of the material in this book was published as 'The Innocence Fetish: The commodification and sexualisation of children in the media and popular culture' in *Media International Australia*, 135 (May 2010), pp. 106–17. I gratefully acknowledge the work of the special issue editors, Catharine Lumby and Kath Albury, as well as anonymous readers, who helped me refine that material.

I would also like to acknowledge that this research has been supported under the Australian Research Council's Discovery Projects funding scheme (project DP0877618). The views expressed herein are mine, and are not necessarily those of the Australian Research Council.

I would like to extend warm thanks to Sarah Maddison, Miriam Bankovsky, Robbie Duschinsky, Ros Diprose, Magdalena Zolkos, Catharine Lumby and Paul Patton for discussing with me elements of the project, and/or reading and advising on drafts of chapters. Thanks also to Jared van Duinen, who provided invaluable research assistance in preparation for writing the book. I am indebted to each of the editorial team at Cambridge Australia – Tony Moore, Susan Hanley, Debbie Lee and Jodie Howell – and to my copy editor Sandra Goldbloom Zurbo, for their patient and thorough advice and support while I readied this book for publication.

Thanks and love to Peter Chen for reading the drafts, doing the dishes, and keeping the children fed and watered. And thanks, finally, to the children – Bridget and Myfanwy – whose words and actions have helped to shape this work.

# Encounters with childhood

*Series Editor Tony Moore*

In recent years no issue has evoked more community passion and angst than the fear that childhood innocence is under threat. Asking difficult questions to uncover truths has always been the philosopher's burden and in *The Importance of Being Innocent*, philosophy scholar Joanne Faulkner does just that with the growing anxiety that the innocence of our children is no longer sacred.

Threats to childhood innocence have been the subject of a succession of moral panics: the commercial exploitation of children; physical and behavioural disorders; the early sexualisation of pre-adolescent 'tweenies'; exposure to media violence and internet porn; child abuse and neglect; and most alarming of all, sexual predation by paedophiles. The other side is a middle-class obsession with perfecting the childhood experience, as 'helicopter' parents with fewer children regulate a regime of value-adding activities and tuition. Faulkner asks if adults in fact fetishise the innocence of children, to compensate for their own feelings of alienation and powerlessness.

Bill Henson's photographs of a young girl on the cusp of puberty disturbed and outraged many Australians, and led to police seizing the offending images. But the furore over these artworks raises the question: why can politicians, interests groups and media invoke the defence of childhood innocence, certain that it will garner widespread community support and silence opposition?

In seeking to understand our anxieties, Faulkner begins with what we mean by childhood innocence and why it is so important to us. How have notions of the child collided with recent changes in our society, especially adults' sense of control over their own lives? It was only in the twentieth century that children in the West were removed from the adult world of toil by the state and confined in the safe havens of the family and school. After tracing Western notions of innocence in myth, religion, literature and philosophy, and discussing enlightenment and romantic idealisations of childhood, Faulkner considers the historical pathways leading to what she deems Australia's particular obsession with innocent children: colonialism and dependence on a 'mother' country; convict transportation and concern to wash away the 'stain'; the dispossession of the Indigenous inhabitants; fear of the environment; and an enacted desire to purify our population from the corruption of the old world, and the non-white foreigners at our doorstep. Faulkner then examines how accelerated economic and social changes over recent decades have left us more insecure in our communities and working lives. In compensation do adults obsess about those over whom they still exercise control – their children? Are children increasingly an extension of adults' own barely articulated needs?

The contemporary ideal of pristine innocence is revealed to be verging on fantasy. What happens to the many children who fail to meet its exacting standards? In much of the world children must work to support their families, and routinely run the gauntlet of poverty, famine, natural disasters, war and tyrannical government. Some children fleeing oppression and crises in developing, war-torn countries breach our borders and comfort zone as refugees, and present a very different image of childhood. What of those local children, both Indigenous and settler, compelled to contend with collapsing communities and arbitrary and at times cruel state surveillance? Children who hang in gangs, who abuse alcohol or other substances, who commit crimes, who harm other children or adults, who have sex, are condemned by media and politicians for delinquency and deviancy.

The ultimately unsuccessful exclusion of children from the adult market economy is mirrored by a legally enforced exclusion from political rights. Working class adults, women and Aborigines were once deemed unable to govern themselves, popular prejudice dismissing them as too childlike to exercise citizen rights such as voting. Thinking laterally about the future trajectory of citizenship and human rights, the author challenges us to take a leap, and consider how our perception and treatment of children might change to enhance Australian democracy.

# Chapter 1
# Why do we worry about children?

## Baby on board

Worrying about children is a national vocation. When I had my first child, I was technically an adult. But I looked young, and remember hearing older women tut tut in the street. 'Look,' they would say, 'children are having children these days.' In many ways I was still a child, as are many first-time parents right up until the moment they stake a claim on the audacious conceit of parenthood: here is a person I am ultimately responsible for, and about whom I will worry until my dying day. This realisation, through which one finally – just in time or perhaps a little too late – takes on the mantle of parenthood, is supposed to extinguish the last remnant of one's own childhood. The moment of worrying about children is, for the parent, adulthood's defining moment. It marks an irrevocable passage: at once an assumption of duty, and the loss of an innocence that, sadly, we didn't know we possessed.

This book is concerned with this relationship between the worry about children and adult identity. Although there are obviously other ways of experiencing adulthood than as a parent, the parent–child axis increasingly regulates our ideals of legitimate social participation. Fear for children and childhood, especially, is a significant feature of contemporary Australian self-awareness. We are aware of the risks posed to children today because these concerns are continually worked over in our newspapers and weekend magazines, on radio and television, and even in parliament. In an increasingly risk-averse and litigious world, ever more attention is paid to the dangers children face in the schoolyard, the local playground and the amusement park. Lately, even the grocery aisle is a source of anxiety – a gingerbread house that lures children to hyperactivity, obesity and an early grave. Children playing in the street outside the family home are prey to roving paedophiles, children watching television are vulnerable to cynical advertisers and suggestive music videos, and children surfing the internet are liable to stumble across pornography, virtual stalkers or bullies. Our modern world appears positively hostile to children, and parents feel acutely vulnerable in the face of the corrupting influences of contemporary culture.

Of course, it is eminently reasonable that parents should want to protect their children. And we can easily comprehend the special consideration given to children's lives over others', such as the sense of fragility that motivates the placing of a baby on board sign in a car window. What is perhaps questionable about the focus on children's vulnerability is our rigid understanding of childhood as unworldly, incapable and pure. Prevailing opinion is not only that children are at risk, but also that childhood itself is in crisis, that children are being denied their childhood, an increasingly secluded, sentimentalised, innocent experience to which they have a special right.

Such lamentation only thinly obscures the claims on childhood of its protectors. My question is: What does childhood mean to us, beyond the rich variety of feelings, attitudes, behaviours and experiences of actual children? Australians hold dear to their belief in a way of being that can be secured from the worries and hang-ups of ordinary life, and children are representatives of such otherworldly existence. We have a stake in innocence, which shapes not only adult, but also Australian identity. The group of individuals who are placeholders for innocence play a crucial part in defining the meaning and value of Australian community. We protect the innocent child because they are vulnerable, but they also act as proxies for our vulnerability. The baby on board sign says that we are important, and not only the child.

Ironically, the Australian investment in innocence has perverse effects for children, who are both valued and resented for the very same reasons, because they represent an escape from the responsibility and tedium of everyday life that is closed to adults. Resentment of children is something to which most adults do not freely admit. Perversely, it usually comes into the open only in relation to children whose circumstances place them beyond the scope of innocence. A barely hidden resentment of teenagers and under-privileged children is directly proportional to the overvaluation of innocence. The importance of innocence permits ignorance of, for instance, the mortality rates of adolescents, which are today fourfold that of small children.[1] Precisely at the point children are seen to lose their innocence, adults forget that they, too, are vulnerable, and so their value to us is also lessened. It is the symbolic equivalence between children, innocence, vulnerability and cultural value that worries us so about children. But what does this worry really signify? And what does the innocent child really mean to us?

## Young and free: the innocent Australian

Although concern for children is rising across the Western world, the chord struck by threats to childhood innocence in Australia is curiously resonant. Politicians, charities and marketers regularly exploit its emotional significance to great effect – to secure our votes, to tweak our consciences or to sell a product. No scandal is greater than the possible violation of a child's innocence, and the more abstract this violation, the more vociferous is Australians' outrage (take the Bill Henson controversy over the portrayal of naked children, which will be discussed in chapter 6). It is innocence that is at issue, and not only children's, but an innocence that also represents a national way of life and a relationship to other nations.

If we look to the founding narratives of Australian identity – stories we continually tell ourselves in search of a national essence – innocence lies at their core, and the privileging of innocence as a defining feature of being Australian is sometimes a remarkably creative achievement. Australians joke that we descend from convicts, for instance, and wear this ignoble origin proudly as indicative of a deep-seated larrikinism. Yet what enables us to rejoice in this status is a firm belief in the innocence of our ancestors' intent: our larrikinism is harmless because they were innocent of any serious crime. Rather, they were victims of poverty in unjust, authoritarian times. This qualification is central to how we perceive our past and its relation to the present.

Other narratives of our origins reaffirm this commitment to innocence, for the most part through tales of abandonment that echo the concern for the vulnerability of children. Britain, the mother country, neglected early Australian settlers, who were placed at the mercy of a harsh, unknown climate and infertile soils. Australia was again abandoned, we tell ourselves, at Gallipoli – our second birth as the innocent progeny of negligent parenthood. But this storyline is evident from the beginning of Australian nationhood. As Richard White argues in *Inventing Australia*,[2] when first forging means of positive self-representation, emerging Australians reached for images of pure and innocent young women and children. Drawn upon by politicians and social reformers, and drawn in cartoons in popular publications such as *The Bulletin*, these pictures of innocence, through which a population came to understand what it means to be Australian, consolidated a sunny, wholesome sense of identity. But they also served to conceal deeper tensions within Australian society – class, gender and racial differences, for instance – and to mobilise a sense of vulnerability to a hostile outside world that defines Australian notions of identity and self-interest even today. Significantly, for Richard White, the first legislation of the newly constituted federal parliament was defensive, enacted to protect a youthful and fragile nation from the yellow peril, predation by aggressive trade partners, and foreign disease.[3] The Australian innocence represented by the image of the young woman or child, then, was inextricably bound to a sense of vulnerability. This figure 'often found herself in difficult situations, modestly blushing at vice, naively shocked at corruption, or in imminent danger of being raped'.[4] The purity of Australia's innocence was connected to her youth, but also to fears of being defiled by foreign interests and (cultural or pathological) contagion.

These national icons of (an imperilled) innocence and purity had emerged from earlier fears and fantasies, already depicted in terms of children's vulnerability. In *The Country of Lost Children*, Peter Pierce demonstrates the powerful hold of fears for children upon the colonial imagination.[5] Pierce documents a remarkable volume of stories about children lost to the hostile Australian bush (*Picnic at Hanging Rock* being one of the more famous). That the natural landscape is liable to swallow up our children suggests a discomfort about our very presence here. These stories, Pierce argues, indicate that at the core of Anglo–Australian identity is a sense of not belonging, and a sense of risk to which this not belonging exposes us. But what else does this identification with the lost, innocent child conceal?

There is an alternative Australian narrative about mislaid children that has only recently found voice, and it threatens to destabilise Australians' easy identification with innocence. The children referred to as the Stolen Generation – Aboriginal children removed from their families by government officials allegedly because of parental neglect – now form a significant component of our national story, a component with which we are yet to come to terms. Emotional investment in the ideal of Australian innocence must always be considered in relation to our forgetting of this critical page of Australian history. Taking their cue from the second line of our national anthem, Australians insist they are young and free, and unlike others on the world stage, without the baggage of history. Our innocence establishes a moral authority – the peculiar acumen of the child who sees the emperor's nakedness, who can call out other nations' hypocrisies and cut through their hedging political correctness. But this claim to an uncomplicated innocence obscures a dense and contested history, about which we protest too much.

Similarly, anxiety about threats to our children's innocence increases as we continue to neglect those children we refuse to see as innocent, because they were never sheltered from life. The unpalatable truth is that the value of a child's innocence depends upon their capacity to be protected. Children born to conditions of poverty or abuse, children who need to work – in short, children deprived of the privilege that would confer innocence upon them – unsettle the parameters of our self-understanding. When we look beyond Australia, the existence of such complicated children signifies a way of life that challenges our own: if someone is to blame it must be their parents, types we would not want to admit to our shores (the children overboard incident will addressed in chapter 5). More locally, we deem underprivileged children threats to childhood innocence more generally, as bad seeds from whom we need to quarantine our own, more fortunate children.

The unfortunate consequences of favouring childhood innocence in our culture are not only borne by children who fall short of this ideal, however. The strictures of innocence limit what even the most privileged of our precious offspring can do and how they can be. This is because innocence performs a social function. The child, embodying innocence, safeguards the innocence of the community. The child is for Australian society a synecdoche – a part that represents the whole[6] – for our most venerable meaning. For this very reason, children's conformity to innocence is closely monitored and worried over. The innocent child, as a figurehead for the innocence of a nation, carries an excessive social burden.

If this cultural trend is left unchecked, and children come to be valued only by virtue of their innocence, we risk losing the capacity to value them in any other respect. It is critical that we begin to explore alternative avenues for understanding and experiencing children. It is hoped that this book will contribute to such a process.

## Innocence in word and deed

In the beginning was the word, and the word was 'innocence.' In Western mythology, life begins innocent and wants to return to innocence, which thereby summarises all that is culturally valuable. Of humble origins, the word 'innocence' derives from the Latin *innocere*: 'to do no harm'. *Innocere* is itself a derivative term, a combination of *in*, meaning 'not', and *nocere*, 'to harm'. We might ask, then, what's so venerable about the quality of doing no harm? How could this negatively defined, insipid concept occupy such a prominent place in the hierarchy of value? And what must a culture have suffered or have feared suffering – what vulnerability must it feel – to so esteem the condition of doing no harm? As we have seen, the innocent, blameless, victim plays a key part in Australia's most potent identity-forming narratives. The power of innocence's resonance for Australian identity in part explains why our relation to children is so decisive. Innocence also features in the imagined prehistory of Western humanity more generally, as even a passing acquaintance with the Old Testament reveals. As we shall see, the place of children in this story of innocence is not as straightforward as it might at first appear.

The Bible begins with Genesis with a narrative of the loss of innocence that defines human being. Adam and Eve are cast out of paradise for disobeying God's only moral law: a prohibition against eating fruit from the tree of knowledge of good and evil. This fall from grace, figured as a fall from heaven to Earth, is a metaphor for the primordial separation from divinity that brings forth human terrestrial life. Humanity is abandoned by God, left to stumble in a desert of uncertainty, to find for itself the right way to live. Not only, then, had a place in paradise been lost, but notably also innocence – and the protection and guidance afforded the inno-cent. After gaining moral knowledge, fallen humanity transitions from innocence to a state of being able to do harm. This loss of innocence is our original sin, an indelible stain of guilt inherited from Adam and Eve as part of the human condition. Innocence had been a state of blissful oneness with God's will. But it is also an unsustainable condition, yielded once one lives in a world rife with harm and compromise. To be agents of one's own life one must cast off innocence. Living a mortal life involves getting one's hands dirty. Or so the story goes.

This story endures through a particular conception of human nature and its possibilities – and importantly, of innocent children as potential, and somewhat ethereal, human beings. Innocence is regarded with a sense of nostalgia, an otherworldly contentment of which mere mortals are unworthy. Our story begins where innocence is already lost, our being already spoiled and broken. This loss not only separates us from our origins, but also drives a constant and tragic effort to rebuild a place of uncorrupted innocence on Earth, and to populate this space with half heavenly, half terrestrial creatures. Such is the social function of childhood. By dint of the story of human meaning in Genesis, children represent what we once were and still ought to be. The story of the fall privileges the innocence children resemble, which apparently belongs to humanity at the point of its origin.

But just as Genesis splits humanity in two – between the exalted and the fallen – our conceptions of children, and the lives they are permitted to live, are also organised by this divide.

This is because innocence so defined is unliveable without an overlord to protect, surveil and control the innocent's every movement. Innocents are secluded from any resources that would enable them to make a decision for themselves. As in the Garden of Eden, the safeguard that ensures incorruptibility is the regulation of information, a control of knowledge that separates innocence from worldliness. After eating the fruit of knowledge, Adam and Eve's fall was inevitable. The maintenance of innocence requires the absence of moral knowledge, as well as of harm and desire. The garden we create for the innocent must be more perfect than

God's: a walled garden, with no snakes and no fruit. To maintain children's innocence, we invent internet filters, censorship regimes and abstinence-only sex education.[7] We rush past billboards advertising longer sex hoping the children won't ask awkward questions. We fear children are not ready developmentally to encounter 'adult themes'. A contamination anxiety is at work here, and a purity fetish for childhood innocence. No everyday issue can be allowed to intrude upon this purity: children must neither know nor experience the kinds of thoughts and feelings the rest take for granted.

In fact, this narrative structure – and the order of values it supports – places children always on the verge of a fall. It allows them to be either angels or fallen angels, either innocence personified or in need of a good spanking. It ignores the broad range of behaviours, opinions and appearances that belong to children but which jar against the ideal of innocence. When adults value the innocence children represent over actual children, they come to downplay aberrant childhood experience so as to maintain this faith. They read behaviour that falls outside the strict parameters of innocence as morally ambiguous – even tending towards evil. This perverse effect of applying the ideal of innocence to children often passes unnoticed. Disadvantaged children, for instance, are regularly depicted as bestial little deviants and prescribed harsh discipline in the guise of tough love. By dressing our children as fairies or in Anne Geddes' originals we momentarily forget how much they enjoy playing in mud, fighting, nose picking and masturbating.

Not so long ago children were seen as little better than untrained animals, and the path to their education and spiritual cultivation was laid with pain. It is not so acceptable to abuse children in the name of their improvement now that we are enlightened to the value of childhood. Yet the physical discipline of children is still an explosive issue today that is regularly ignited in the popular media, as the recent New Zealand referendum about smacking demonstrates.[8] The idea of their inherent goodness slips easily into disgust and violence in the face of bad behaviour. This dissonance produces the spectre of the monstrous child, which huddles in the long shadow cast by innocent childhood. Stories of child bullies, torturers and murderers are so darkly fascinating because through them we can dwell upon ambivalence felt towards children when they don't conform to innocence. These opposing views of children – as either natural innocents or harbourers of original sin – take root in the same soil, according to the rationale of the fall. They do not belong so much to different epochs as to different moments of the same cultural formation of childhood innocence. There must always be failures, children who fall short of such a demanding ideal. A commitment to upholding the innocence of childhood, then, may not best serve children's interests.

## The importance of innocence in the social imaginary

The story of Genesis is so culturally potent that it still influences secular views of social relations and identity. These narratives structure ways of seeing and valuing, and have concrete effects for individuals within a social group. The Edenic story contributes to what's called the 'social imaginary': the stock of images, metaphors, rituals and symbols through which we are able to negotiate a shared understanding of the world.[9] We borrow from a repertoire of signs and practices that are culturally constrained, 'mapping' the social sphere so that others know what our actions mean and their behaviour can make sense to us. The biblical primal scene informs assumptions about the innocence we lost there, and behaviour in relation to that loss. We do not cease telling varieties of this story. A modern iteration, Nabokov's *Lolita*, brings out our ambivalences about innocent children in telling ways.

*Lolita* is a fractured love story told from the perspective of a middle-aged paedophile, about his infatuation with a 12 year old girl. Nabokov invites the reader to identify with its monstrous protagonist, to see from his perspective, but also to see within Humbert Humbert's narration the gaps in his own conscious knowledge and his control of the scene. Peeking through these gaps is Lolita's own point of view, which Humbert at once conceals from himself and reveals to the reader. The logic of the fall organises Humbert's flawed perspective, as he ambiguously positions himself as predator and protector (he is Lolita's stepfather and, after her mother's death, her only guardian). While it is clear it is never Humbert whom Lolita desires, he situates her as a fallen angel or nymphet, vaguely complicit in his sexual abuse by virtue of her desirability. Humbert cites Lolita's precocious experimentation with other children, her interest in Hollywood celebrity and her penchant for an arousing style of dress, as proof of her knowledge of her appeal. But it is ultimately Lolita's unknowingness, or innocence, that Humbert desires, and the uncertain equivocation between naivety and awareness (innocence and guilt) that keeps him enthralled. Her curiosity, and essential vulnerability to corruption, connects Lolita to Eve. Nabokov further links Humbert's perception of Lolita to Genesis by repeatedly observing within the narrative Lolita's half-eaten 'Eden-red' apples. Lolita – modern, insouciant, and 'experienced' – was primed for a fall. All Humbert had to do was hand her the apple.

I've taken this detour through *Lolita* to highlight our culture's volatility of judgement about innocence, to the extent that it is framed through an all too easily lost purity. The stories, or cultural mythologies, through which we tell ourselves who we are, provide structures through which others appear to be easily recognisable. Heroes, villains and innocent victims to be rescued populate these stories, which are punctuated by their various stages of (moral) development. The contemporary equation of innocence with childhood places children in an invidious position. Situated at the beginning of the social narrative they represent purity, but are also potential victims carefully watched for signs of corruption. When placed at the end of this narrative, they become signs of portent about society's future direction, fallen children, emblematic of a degenerate culture, and invested with all the fear and hatred this fate provokes. 'Lolita' is currently shorthand for an unwitting sexual precocity of young girls in search of adult approval. Cautionary tales of corrupted innocents exert a particular fascination – re-enacting as they do the fall through which we have come to make sense of our social world and identity.

It is this story of innocence, however, that sets children up for a fall. We are captured by its movement, and the child, as its emblem, acts as a counterbalance for adult identity. We tell our own identity and desire through these stories about children. If we want to be able to recognise children apart from this bleak narrative – as people with their own thoughts, feelings and perspectives rather than as emblems of downfall – we will need to adopt a critical regard upon the stories that inform cultural value.

## The imaginary economy of innocence: children overboard?

The walled garden we construct for children ensures the sense of moral stability we crave. But it also produces a stable field of social value, a cultural gold standard in the figure of the innocent child. Controlled childhood creates a political economy in which innocence holds the premium value and in which social status depends on one's stock of innocence (often measured in terms of holdings in children). To establish standing as an opinion holder, or to confer urgency upon any issue, one need only say, 'As a parent...' or 'Think of the children'. To those making these claims, the value of childhood appears transparently obvious. In truth, the hype that surrounds childhood obscures the political nature of those claims and the interests they represent.

The social cost of this optimisation of innocence is a restriction of movement for children and young people as well as other members of the community whose relation to them is indirect or complex. Parents and non-parents are accorded a different status on the basis of their proximity to a little bundle of innocence. The model Australian citizen today is the parent of two to three children, with enough income to support them. Successive governments have practised 'natal nationalism' since the Second World War in the name of impending economic crises. Hence former Treasurer Peter Costello's plea to 'have one [baby] for mum, one for dad, and one for the country'.[10] This appeal was aimed at cushioning the economy against the effects of an aging population. Yet there is good reason to believe that, in Australia, having children is considered intrinsically virtuous – and being childless by choice, suspicious and selfish (Senator Bill Heffernan, for instance, questioned Julia Gillard's fitness for leadership on the basis of her being 'deliberately barren').[11] That birth rates increased after Treasurer Costello's suggestion indicates that his bid was in line with conventional Australian values.[12]

Challenging this view of the value and political utility of childhood would involve redistributing our social investments – putting into question what we find worthy, and who can have social currency. As these values are deeply embedded in our social imaginary, such redistribution will require an exercise of the imagination. But imagination is most usually regarded as a child's domain. It is children's prerogative to believe in make-believe things, and adults only enjoy the magical world of childhood at one remove, through their enjoyment. Adults enhance and engineer children's enjoyment of imaginary worlds with fairytales, Santa Claus, the Easter bunny and the tooth fairy. We indulge the child's vivid imagination – and thereby our own enjoyment of a world in which we would like to believe, a world in which dreams come true and life's dreary necessities cannot intrude. But this conflation of childhood with imagination – and the view that imagination escapes reality – leads to two fundamental errors.

First, we miss the important task of imagination in making sense of experience. We fail to comprehend, that is, how our everyday interactions with others, social institutions and our physical environment, are mediated by the imaginary representations we bring to these exchanges. These representations emotionally and conceptually orient us to the world, and affect the relative desirability of situations we encounter. Imagination provides the frame by which we evaluate truth and falsity, and so does not settle on one side of this opposition, as illusion instead of reality. Imagination is instead a crucial resource for the promotion of cultural change.

Second, by coupling imagination with childhood we not only trivialise the imagination, but we also trivialise children. We are led to regard children's experiences as less real, and as less important, than adults' – even as we elevate them above the pettiness of everyday life. By hiving off imagination from reality – and then fusing it with an innocent, sentimentalised childhood – we reinforce the idea that children are too fragile for the harsh vicissitudes of daily life. This approach to childhood is symptomatic of a fearful relation to the sociopolitical situation. Having insufficient imagination to change reality, we charge children with this task by imagining them as otherworldly creatures – as ciphers for creativity and transformation.

Perhaps unsurprisingly, the present crisis of childhood innocence is felt most acutely in relation to the vehicle of cultural representations – popular media – that expose children to sexuality and represents them as sexual objects. But the innocence crisis does not simply signal the demise of a particular mode of childhood experience, although this is how the situation is framed. Rather, we are experiencing a crisis in the value of innocence, which speaks to the very currency of our political economy and the structure of Australian identity (how we imagine our place, our purpose and our future). The media are speculating on the value of innocence, reflecting upon innocence, thereby exposing it to risk in pursuit of profit. Such speculation is a betrayal of our most precious cultural resource – although narratives of harmed children and exploitative adults do not quite capture what's at stake. The image of the child is invested with the role of virtual humanity, and with a purity of essence that enables us to project into it all our hopes and fears about the direction of society. That the child's innocence is undermined compromises its value as a critical component of the social imaginary. We are experiencing a crisis, then, of the imagination, of how we envisage our future and meaning. This centrality of the image of innocent childhood is why attempts to simply deflate apocalyptic claims about the sexualisation of children, the ubiquity of paedophilia or childhood obesity make such little impact on levels of public anxiety (see chapter 2).

Keeping in mind the child's leading role in how we imagine society and human life, I have organised this book around three critical axes: media representations of children, philosophical representations of political man and representations of children who defy our political imagination – who trouble our preconceptions about childhood innocence and so drop out of the innocence matrix. Confronted with the spectre of the child on the verge of corruption or violation, the importance of innocent children to contemporary political life is, paradoxically, their depoliticising effect. While children represent a purity unsoiled by politics, they have also become the face of a politics emptied of political interest. The presence of the child in political life signals a double manoeuvre: because innocent children are encoded as the most important node of social life, it has become *de rigueur* of political strategy that the most socially divisive actions are taken in the name of the child. This strategy silences political opposition: we are given the choice of either toeing the line or revealing a callous disregard for children. The importance of innocence is so culturally indisputable that dissent is easily quashed, with little chance of critical reappraisal, as long as we are entreated to think of the children. We are so emotionally attuned to this plea that our critical faculties are powerless in the face of the spectre of vulnerable childhood – our new fundamentalism.

Chapter 2, then, will explore and evaluate the conceptual divide between childhood innocence and adulthood: how it is maintained – as well as how it breaks down – through beliefs about the behaviours, activities and attitudes considered proper to these stages of life. Children's relation to work and play will be asked after – What kind of work is it acceptable for children to do? – as will how our intense commitment to the value of child play serves a cultural system we also feel exploits children. Chapter 2 continues the investigation begun here of the hidden value of innocent childhood by framing our deeply felt opinions about children in terms of adult interests and hypocrisies.

Chapter 3 turns to the assumptions about childhood embedded in political notions of what it is to be human, for instance, what kind of agency (ability to alter the world) or citizenship (capacity to participate) is available to children, given the idealised and limited notions of childhood assumed by political theory. Can the child be both a citizen and the citizen's raw material? But further, the chapter explores the complex connection between the cultural meaning of childhood and current limits to notions of citizenship, in order to address our impoverished experience of democracy. The burning question is not whether we should extend the vote to children, but rather what practices other than voting comprise democracy. By interrogating children's relation to how we understand the political and freedom, we may find the resources to become more active – and more critical – citizens.

Chapter 4 examines the historical dimension of the truths we take for granted when talking about children's interests, the development of the knowledges and practices through which we frame the essence of childhood. The chapter will probe the assumption that the character of childhood exists outside a historical–political–social context and situates childhood within the milieu that nowadays tends to define our freedoms: the family. The chapter will develop the idea pursued in chapter 2 that Western citizenship is moulded in terms of a (repudiated) relation to children.

Chapter 5 will consider those children most betrayed by the preoccupation with innocence as the descriptor of childhood. It argues that adolescents, children seeking political asylum and Aboriginal children are particularly marginalised because they fail to conform to our images of what childhood should be. Additionally, this betrayal occurs most insidiously through the direct application of such images of innocent childhood: where images of children are invoked cynically to channel public sentiment against the very communities that can support them. Reports of children overboard and the abused children of the Northern Territory are exaggerated, taken out of context and sometimes even invented in order to depoliticise their situations. Yet the effect of this manoeuvre is to more deeply politicise childhood. Applying the label 'innocence' in such cases allows us to waver between wilfully ignoring their material situations and regarding them as a lost cause (because they are already fallen).

Chapter 6 returns us to the hearth on which our representations of childhood innocence are forged – to the social imaginary through which we might find new ways to critique and reorganise the meaning of childhood. The relation of art to childhood – and particularly the significance of Bill Henson's photographs of adolescent nudity – is re-examined in the light of the importance of childhood innocence to social experience and Australian identity. Opportunities for further thought that Henson's speculations on childhood provide will be opened out. For although we might baulk at the uncertainty art and media controversies produce, it is possible – even desirable – that there might be a social profit from the crisis in the value of innocence they open up. Through this crisis, new understandings of what childhood means and what children are capable of may be formed, understandings that might be of greater interest to the children themselves.

But more than this: these representations of childhood that most trouble us also bring us face to face with a sleight of hand that governs our relationship to childhood. This subterfuge involves passing off our own helplessness as the child's, rendered as ultimately vulnerable. For this reason, if we are to improve conditions for children, we also need to confront ourselves with this disturbing significance of our worry about them, worry through which we manage our vulnerability by exerting a power over children's modes of behaviour and self-expression. This redirection of vulnerability into the child speaks to current anxieties about citizenship and democracy. Because true liberal democracy involves risk: the risk of disclosing one's desires and the risk of being vulnerable to the desires of others.

Despite our love for children, then, the importance of innocence has little to do with their welfare, and a great deal to do
with adults' discomfort in the world. But if innocence is not the all-
important element of childhood, then how are we to understand
children, to protect them and support them? We can begin by
recognising the cultural meaning for all of us of helpless, innocent
childhood. Thinking through this conceptual knot might enable us
to take responsibility for contemporary social, political and ecolog-
ical predicaments.

# Chapter 2
# Consuming the innocent
## Innocence as a cultural and political product

## The innocence fetish

It's a curious truth of contemporary culture that, as innocence has come to be associated with childhood, children are increasingly fetishised. Nothing illustrates this more starkly than the child beauty pageant. A multibillion dollar industry in the United States,[1] child pageantry is the meeting place of a range of ideas about the promise children represent to society: carefree and playful, beautiful and affluent, sublime and unblemished, patriotic and pure of heart. Yet the hard work girls put into their performances and the sacrifices they make to attain them undercut these venerable meanings. For their parents and the pageant industry these children can be lucrative earners. This presents cognitive dissonance. Innocence is not supposed to be useful; it is a value that most feel should transcend profit or personal gain.

More than this, the peddling of children's innocence on the stage or catwalk is seen to place them in danger. The case of JonBenét Ramsey, the six year old beauty queen whose murder shocked and outraged the world in 1996, underscores this sentiment. The daughter of a former Miss West Virginia, JonBenét enjoyed a degree of success on the child pageant circuit, but was unknown to the general public before her brutal (and unsolved) murder.[2] JonBenét's parents and the pageant industry were put on trial by media for objectifying and sexualising this young girl. It was generally agreed that, had she been able to lead the life of a normal six year old, JonBenét would have remained safely ensconced in her cocoon of innocence. The police suspected the parents of her murder. At the very least, as guardians of that innocence, her parents must have been to blame.

The aggressor against children's 'natural' innocence is often seen to be commercial interests and a commodity culture that cheapens and exploits children's beauty. If we look closer, however, we find that an increasingly ambiguous childhood innocence is the hottest commodity on the market. Images of JonBenét in the full garb of pageantry flooded our television screens and the pages of our newspapers – we could not tear our eyes away from them. We like to say that childhood innocence ought to be quarantined from commercial exploitation, but something within us is also animated by others' imperilled innocence: adults have a stake in preserving the innocence of children, through whom we imagine our own possibilities and understand our own selves as surely as any pageant parent. We want our own piece of innocence, packaged in just the way we've learnt to consume it – complete with a use-by date of around 12 years of age.

In the light of these contradictions, many see the child beauty pageant as morally and aesthetically dubious. A *reductio ad absurdum* to the values of contemporary society, these pageants ironically stage the contradictions and grossest excesses of popular culture. The child pageant is the tipping point at which innocence becomes sexual, where beauty becomes garish and cuteness obscene. But what if the contest represented by the pageant is not between innocence and other, more mercantile, values that put it at risk? What if, rather, the contradictions that the pageant reveals belong to innocence itself? What if the desirability of innocence sets in train the very behaviours and subcultures that threaten it? And if, precisely by setting innocence apart from the commerce of everyday life, we increase its commercial value?

The commercialisation of childhood innocence that child pageantry represents can be understood as a particularly unpalatable aspect of a quite ordinary regard for children. Critics of the movement might say that childhood is a special time of innocence, that children should be allowed to be children. But pageantry's proponents would reply that they couldn't agree more, that children's innocence is celebrated by the pageants – which are fun, that their girls are just doing what children love. Whatever constitutes children just being children is an empty enough prescription that child pageants can claim to fill it. The saccharine images of children that they produce draw upon, and contribute to, the very same tradition of imagining childhood innocence in whose name many of the industry's critics speak.

## The Australian context

In Australia, too, there has recently been a marked increase in public attention to the commercial use and representation of children. On one hand, it is feared children are now targets of a range of products that were once off limits to them: make-up, fragrances, adult styles of clothing and a cool, sexualised insouciance that was formerly associated with teenagerhood. On the other hand, advertisers' use of child actors and models is gaining notice, most especially the use of children to sell products consumed by adults. Policy think tank the Australia Institute, has claimed that by employing children to sell products associated with adult pleasure – and by making them adopt behaviours, poses and the accoutrements of adulthood – the media sexualise children, thereby placing them at risk. This risk is rhetorically personified by the figure of the paedophile, for which our media groom children by normalising sexual comportments and clothing.[3]

This has become such a concern that in 2008 the Senate conducted an inquiry into the sexualisation of children in the contemporary media environment. The inquiry recommended that the advertising industry self-regulator overhaul its existing standards of practice.[4] The Australia Institute reports have come under fire for the carelessness of this research.[5] Nonetheless they provided a rallying point around which concerned politicians, the media and child protection activists could coalesce. They also provided the language of family values fused with a critique of corporate morality that now characterises this discussion.[6]

Yet despite the din of voices expressing concern for children, once the sound is turned down what we see is a fascination with the sexual child. The child has become titillating to the point where the paedophile's gaze is privileged over all others, as we search for signs of sexual precocity in every brochure advertising preteen fashion. Paedophiles represent a risk to children, to be sure, and recent revelations about the scope of child abuse in the church and other institutions are alarming. But to foreground paedophilia in discussions of children's reception of media seems at best melodramatic, at worst to trivialise the experience of victims of actual child abuse.[7] Something else is at work here, at the level of psychological identification. The paedophile–advertiser and the moral guardian are engaged in a staring match that does not so much signal a conflict as it does a perverse complicity. The baseline assumption for both the paedophile and the protector is that the child's body is essentially sexual. For critics such as Hamilton, Rush and Devine, children are prone to inflame sexual feeling in adults unless restricted to specific contexts that frame them as innocent, contexts that are apparently disappearing, connected as they are with our own lost childhood – a bygone era before the world was corrupted by violence, sex and greed.[8] In a climate in which a fully clothed child pictured slumped in a leather armchair is sexualised because she is in an adult setting,[9] we must conclude that the readiness to view children as sexual is not only the affliction of paedophiles and pornographers.

This is not to say that Hamilton, the Senate, Rudd and child protection advocates such as Hetty Johnson get their secret jollies from the commercial exploitation of children. I think they do sincerely hold the belief that they represent the best interests of children. But given the focus of their criticisms, they surely get something out of children's sexualisation, whether a sense of vital importance to the community, political mileage with their electorate or, more fundamentally, reassurance that they are good parents (and, thereby, good citizens). Childhood innocence sells for the same reason we feel it should be protected from commercial interests. Advertisers – like advocates for pageants – push the envelope with their representations of adorable, desirable children. But what they bring to the surface is a cultural undercurrent through which all that is valued – and desired – is represented by the child.

## Innocence as the premium cultural commodity

As our cultural mythology would have it, a cherubic child will one day redeem society. Whether baby Jesus or little Eppie (in George Eliot's *Silas Marner*), Bindi Irwin or Nullah (in Baz Luhrmann's *Australia*), the child heralds our salvation, conceived as a redemptive return to a lost, primordial innocence.

The power of this myth was brought home to me recently at a school award night. As often happens, a local member of parliament was asked to speak, bestowing on a struggling school social legitimacy by witnessing the achievements of its students. Her contribution to the pomp of the evening was the kind of pro forma talk everyone has heard time and again: 'You children are our future. We adults have already ruined everything. Now it's up to you to set it right.' A heavy chalice to pass any 10th grader. At the time I was struck by the casual manner in which this member of the political elite was allowed to wipe her hands of the sins of a generation.

(Before the awards could be distributed the member was promptly called away to more urgent business.)

The child as protocitizen is thus inducted into this cultural mythology as the redemptive power of innocence. Because they are yet to be contaminated by the selfish and perverse desires of adults, they are fit to make the sacrifices the rest of us have been unable to make: recycling, eating less, exercising more, using public transport, saving the whales and otherwise selflessly salvaging the world from the destruction wrought by their profligate parents. Children have the healing power to remedy the tainted harvest of adults' ineptitude and thereby to absolve us of our guilt and our sins. The child's power is thus conceived in the model of divinity, as our sacred absolution.

Yet once blemished by social problems, the child comes to embody them: as they can't possibly live up to such an idealised image, children easily slip from their pedestal. In discussions about the ills of society, the focus given to children offers an even more dubious absolution to adults. Children are too lazy, materialistic, cynical, promiscuous, fat. 'Obesity epidemic now affecting babies', screams one headline, as the prospect of child services removing overweight children from their families is floated for readers' delectation.[10] We're all going to hell in a hand basket because the sins of parents are magnified in their children. It's getting to the point where endemic social problems are visible only insofar as they affect children.

The difference between Lolita and Shirley Temple, then, is their place within the cultural mythology of innocence. While Temple and her ilk exist in an eternal state of innocent desirability, and so retain the promise of a better world to come, Lolita reveals the fragility of this desirable innocence (which all too easily verges into sexuality and corruption), and the extent to which we are all implicated in her wretchedness. Despoiled innocence is the monstrous by-product of a culture that glorifies an innocent, unknowing and inexperienced childhood. Not only does this model of childhood fail to prepare children for the threats from which we wish to protect them, but the notion of a pristine innocence, separate from the kinds of human interactions through which knowledge and experience are gathered, is also quite impossible. The child must at some point be exposed to life's harsher vicissitudes; it is a matter of cultural prejudice whether this event is interpreted as a fall, a necessity or a period of growth.

The child who is not maintained in a state of innocence is fallen, and a grim reminder of life's difficulties and disappointments. The despoiled innocent – children who are abused or in poverty, who have to work, or are otherwise excluded from the sanctuary of 'normal' childhood – is seen as a warning sign that society is failing in its charter to protect the innocent. Viewed from another direction, perhaps what it actually signals is that children are valued to the extent that they are able to support an ideal of innocence attainable only through great wealth and privilege. While JonBenét Ramsey's was a highly conspicuous death, every day there are many less glamorous child casualties of commercial society that are overlooked. While these deaths are often seen as inevitable, and are far too numerous for Western consciences to bear, what distinguishes a girl such as JonBenét is the perceived preventability of her death. A white, middle-class American girl, she had a future. More than that, she *was* the future: the sum of consumer culture's aspirations crystallised in the sparkle of her pretty blue eyes. The brutality of her murder – together with the perceived brutality of the pageant circuit – generated such anxiety because JonBenét's privilege reflected our own hopes and dreams for the future. Her vulnerability, in turn, revealed the stakes of the fetishisation of innocence for Western, consumerist culture. What the case of JonBenét Ramsey brought into view was the material conditions through which the ideal of innocence is produced, and this revelation ultimately debased its fetish value. Hence our discomfort.

We can gain insight into the power of the beauty pageant if we look to German political philosopher Karl Marx's economic theory. In the 19th century, and in the context of the emergence of the capitalist market, Marx was concerned about what he saw as the alienation of human labour. Marx explained his concept of commodity fetishism in terms of a curious phenomenon of every-day economic life, whereby we value goods independently of the conditions of their production or their use – and importantly for Marx – the commodity eclipses the relationships between people that ought to give that object meaning. A commodity fetish, such as a luxury car, is attributed an almost magical ability to increase the status of its owner. Its value is based on this socially inscribed power rather than the value of the work and materials that were invested in making it, or the use to which it is put. This fetish value is also reflected in what the Norwegian–American economist Thorstein Veblen identified in the early 20th century as 'conspic-uous consumption'.[11] The commodity fetish, or 'Veblen good', is valuable because of what it costs. The object's meaning is elevated above its use: its value is purely symbolic, because possessing it signifies one's wealth or cultural acumen.

The power of the beauty pageant, for those who are entranced by it, is that it raises these little girls to perfect exemplars of fem-ininity, without revealing the means by which this transformation was achieved. If we can set aside the many hours of voice and dance training, of driving from pageant to pageant, of putting on make-up, whitening teeth and practising the perfect smile, then the beauty queen child will embody for us the ideal of innocence. This ideal, however, is a commodity fetish. We exaggerate its value only because we are able to overlook the concrete circumstances of its production. While JonBenét was a beauty queen we could believe that she was innocence personified, that her image coin-cided with the ideals it represented. It was only after her death that the schism within that image erupted and viewers' cognitive dissonance was revealed. What fascinated viewers of these perfect images as they were showcased on the news was the chasm that had opened for them between the ideals they represented and the reality they obscured.

Similarly, for those not enchanted by the beauty pageant – for whom, indeed, it is a transparently exploitative practice – the child as commodity fetish is already debased by the pageant. The pageant is found to be garish because it stages innocence too crudely and fails adequately to conceal the conditions by which it is enacted. Disdain for the child pageant thus expresses a middle-class sense of distinction that French sociologist Pierre Bourdieu calls 'cultural capital': a know-how regarding the origins and meanings of cultural products that marks one out as having more refined tastes than others. Bourdieu developed Marx's theory of commodity fetishism to show how a sense of one's social place can be articulated in terms of the products (food, clothes, films, etc.) one will or will not consume. Bourdieu's point is exemplified well by the hit comedy series *Kath and Kim*, in a face-off between the show's title characters and their more refined (that is, snobbish) bourgeois alter egos, Prue and Trude.

**Prue**  How about something in your Bodum?

**Kim**  I beg yours!

**Prue**  A plunger in your Bodum's always nice. And it
comes with these matching cups which are cyuuute.

**Kim**  Nuh.

The comic element of this encounter is the extent to which Kath/Prue and Kim/Trude are fundamentally the same – played, as they are, by the same actors – but identify themselves as essentially different by dint of their consumer decisions. Their understanding of self and of others is mediated by a cultural literacy that is experienced as natural and broadly seen as a matter of taste.

Following Bourdieu, then, the beauty pageant offends educated middle-class people because its codes are easily read, rendering the production of childhood innocence too visible. Once the circumstances of its cultural production are obvious, the innocent child, who instead takes on the visage of the sexual coquette, no longer enchants. But the beauty pageant is not different in kind from other, more proficient – or perhaps more class appropriate – performances of innocence that middle-class consumers readily approve: Dakota Fanning's (Lucy's) blind faith in her developmentally delayed father in *I Am Sam*, for instance, or Drew Barrymore's much vaunted charm in portraying Gertie, who befriends the ultimate stranger, an alien, in *E.T.* These performances were manufactured with sweat and tears just as surely as JonBenét's were. But we do not find middle-class parents boycotting all films that use child labour – far from it. We all hang out for our fix of childhood innocence.

This element of class distinction played out in relation to the representation of innocence (questions of taste regarding whether one prefers viewing children in pageantry or cinematic make-up), also explains the sense of outrage when these bourgeois constructions of childhood innocence are themselves read – as occurred recently when Catherine Deveny tweeted 'I so do hope Bindi Irwin gets laid' (so ending her career at the *Age*). Just as Gertie's, or Bindi's or even JonBenét's innocent image is the product of hard graft and social mythology, the innocence of our own children is also manufactured. It is manufactured by virtue of the ideals acted out by the adorable child actor and is manufactured through social arrangements that obscure and even prevent children's involvement in everyday life. Childhood innocence is manufactured using the enormous resources available to Western citizens so that they are able to withdraw children from the circuit of economic production altogether[12] (sequestering them into schools, where their work produces a reserve of human capital[13] that is only superficially kept separate from the rest of society).[14] By being able to have children who do not labour with us, children's resources are kept in potential for the production of our highest cultural values. Once children have no use value – becoming instead precious economic liabilities – they become fetishes. Their exalted, fetish value is a direct consequence of their apparent distance from economic concerns. Children seem to emanate from a pure desire, unpolluted by worldly needs. We protect our children, value them above all other humanity, precisely insofar as they are not useful, and have not yet lived. Because their work, unlike that of children in the developing world or of the past, is not put to use, our children are innocent and so notionally more worthy.

Yet what characterises the innocence of fictional children such as Lucy and Gertie, and real children such as JonBenét, is their vulnerability. The innocent is the one who does no harm and so is positioned as the one who is defenceless and most susceptible to harm. Calamity, and a fall, is the inevitable outcome of such vulnerability, engendered through the ideal of innocence. What is sacrificed to this ideal is a childhood through which children are allowed to learn through experience and partake – albeit in a modified way – in the activities and contexts that feature in adult life. Such is the condition of a growth and agency that, by means of the myth of childhood innocence, children are deprived.

## Where will the children play? Play as a focus of adult desire and anxiety

Quite paradoxically, the site of much anxiety about threats to the innocence of children is also recognised as the foremost privilege of childhood: play. Play is one of the only socially approved means available to children by which they can interpret their world. Play is how children work through the diverse, confusing and inconsistent cultural experiences they face each day. Play also carries considerable cultural baggage for adults. We, who have had to put down our toys, are often ambivalent about play. We carry within us the remnants of a puritanical purge of recreation that accompanies the rise of a protestant work ethic.[15] Also, we may harbour justified qualms about play as the niche of our lives through which the capitalist economy takes its irrevocable hold upon us. This contradiction, between the repression of play (required for production) and the incitement to play (required for consumption), means that the good citizen of a capitalist democracy must suspend enjoyment (citizen as producer) and party hard (citizen as consumer – 'Let's spend our way out of this recession'). This double bind creates uneasiness about play in general, as the source of both guilt and reward. It also creates uneasiness about children who, insofar as they are given sanction to play, are also envied.

This means children's play attracts a fascination in adults that reflects such emotional dissonance. It is generally agreed that children must be children – meaning they must be allowed to play – because we must be adults. We redress the imbalance of our intensely productive lives by sacrificing our enjoyment to them. Our envy of the playful child, and grim determination that they must have fun on our behalf, expresses itself in perverse and distorted ways. At any one time some form or other of child play is viewed as immoral or dangerous – 'Dungeons and Dragons', for instance, thought in the 1980s, when the game's popularity was at its peak, to lead to devil worship and witchcraft, just as are computer games and social networking today, which are feared to cause childhood obesity and impaired thought, and expose children to internet predators. Children, then, are imperilled even by the play that is their entitlement as children. Does this merely echo the puritan suspicion that idle hands are the devil's playthings? Or is there something more complicated and profound at work here, something connected to adult identity and desire?

## A brief history of play

If sex, politics and work are defining activities of adulthood, play is considered the preserve of childhood, one aspect of life that sets children apart. Yet once there was no distinction made between the leisure activities and toys of children and adults – indeed, the boundary between adulthood and childhood was more porous than it is taken to be today[16] (as coming of age rites demonstrate, such as the Jewish Bar and Bat Mitzvah, respectively for 13 year old boys and 12 year old girls).

Since the industrial revolution – and the creation of a private sphere, kept apart from the productive workplace – play has become increasingly associated with children. Play is unproductive, and so in a culture that values productivity, is discouraged. Children, however, are valued insofar as they represent the inverse of adulthood. What makes us good as adults is that we can support an unproductive burden. Children (and formerly women) embody the values of our culture – including its work ethic – to the extent that their use value is underrated and set aside. By remaining excluded from work and the everyday concerns of adulthood, children, prior to socialisation, preserve in the social imagination a life of pure enjoyment. The mixed feelings we have about what this mythologised presocial existence would involve will be explored in chapter 3. We indulge fantasies that it would be pleasurable, but also fears of its potential violence or destabilising effects. Without social agreement about right and wrong behaviour, we can envisage much brutality: the dark side of play projected onto other people's children, who are liable to bully our own. Child play is invested with these fantasies of excessive enjoyment and aggression that are the flip side of a life given over to social demands and responsibilities.

Through the notion of child play, children are endowed with what's come to be the mandate of contemporary life. They represent the liberty, pleasure and fulfilment that is (at least rhetorically) the goal of all Western democracies, a goal that is substantially indistinguishable from that of late capitalism, for which enjoyment is conceivable only in terms of consumption. At a cultural rather than economic level, play is the sign of what Marx called 'surplus value': the excess that ultimately renders all our work and toil profitable.[17] To be able to watch our children play after a hard day's work – isn't that what gives a good parent's life meaning? The pure happiness of children, unadulterated by the necessities of life, that child play represents, apparently makes the alienation of adult labour worthwhile. Children embody a conspicuous leisure that Veblen identified as a universal signifier of social success: they are allowed to play because they are precious, and precious because they represent the last vestige of leisure we all desire.

Yet since the first institution of a cleavage between adult and juvenile modes of recreation, play in children's lives has also been a principal object of worry and surveillance. Where children play, with what and whom, and the safety of play are often points of contention, for children and society as a whole. Presently, we worry that, for instance, children's play is not active enough, that children are too absorbed in virtual worlds that do not sufficiently exercise the body or the mind and that these games promote violence and erode morals. In recent years public space has also become a stage upon which anxieties about children's playful activities are acted out. The surveillance of children's recreation has been a concern for elderly residents, shop owners and local business people who decry the presence of children aimlessly hanging out in what they classify as a commercial – and therefore productive – domain. As will be considered in greater depth in chapter 5, extraordinary legal and physical efforts are expended to regulate children's activities in public spaces, and to deter them from congregating there.

From the beginning of modernity the task of delimiting the spaces in which children play has been motivated by commercial interests, albeit in the name of protecting them from the violence of adult (and commercial) life. Indeed, the separation of children from productive work to the world of play, learning and leisure is a relatively recent event that occurred in tandem with the rise of the capitalist economy in the 19th century, and was precipitated by a contest of the values that define childhood itself. In the first decades of the 20th century, Western children were gradually removed from the workplace, and education became the universal standard occupation of children. This event was an advance for children's welfare, and the industrial law reforms that enabled it protected children from the dangers of heavy machinery and hard labour. Yet these benefits to children, obvious today, were not so evident at the time. A revolution in the meaning of childhood was taking place, a change from the view that work was good for children and nothing was worse than an idle child, to the now predominant belief that childhood is a time for recreation and children are too precious to be put to use (to the extent that today many have qualms about extracurricular coaching for children to attain entry to selective state schools, which is seen as something Asian immigrants do, as well as putting children to work in shops, again considered a feature of ethnic businesses).

For the working-class people most affected by child labour reforms, there was no clear advantage to sending their children to school, which at best meant a loss of perhaps a third of annual household income, at worst additional expense.[18] In the 1920s and 1930s in Australia, working-class parents who withheld their children from schooling were prosecuted, while in the UK children were bribed with the promise of a hot lunch. These reforms caused considerable hardship and painful adjustment for such families. In the meantime, these social upheavals supported the growth of industry by producing a new pool of skilled labour fit for a new, more technological economy. The exclusion of children from the workforce coincided with commercial interests in new social arrangements, such as the enlargement of the private sphere and an increased sanctity of the family. Children, safe in the home, helped to create the now familiar notion of the family as the focus of enjoyment, security and satisfaction. The family had come of age as the ultimate engine of consumption.

Commercial interests further delimited the zone of play, as the first automobile users and manufacturers conducted a turf war with children over the streets. This bloody struggle culminated in what we now understand as a natural arrangement: children play in playgrounds and backyards, not on roads. At one time children, adult pedestrians, horsedrawn carriages and trams shared roads with cars. Indeed, it was motorists who were considered the intruders, and many parents defended children's right to play on the street. Only mounting casualties and a persistent public relations offensive by automobile users and manufacturers changed perceptions about the 'proper place' of children.[19] A playground movement, initiated by health advocates and funded by business groups (including automobile interests), built play areas especially for children and educated them that the road is no place to play.[20]

Today we are so used to children being kept apart that their presence in public causes anxiety. Public space is adult space. Divided between adult leisure spaces such as cafés, bars and shopping centres, public space is now largely in private – commercial – owner-ship that is unwelcoming of children and youths. While teenagers are pushed to the margins – to car lots, parkland and alleyways between buildings – or to niche commercial spaces such as arcades, younger children must be under constant adult supervision. Even walking alone to school is now frowned upon; parents deliver their children, courier-like, door to door. These concerns for children's safety sit alongside the fear of adolescent delinquency. The young person sighted in public is recognised only as at risk, or as the risk itself.

## From little rascals to little angels: the meaning of play

This moral weight given to children's presence in public is asso-ciated with anxiety about exploitation: in theory, if the child is cosseted in a domestic haven, they are less vulnerable to the brutal-ities of commercial and political life. Separation, however, is coun-terproductive, and we will consider the intimate relation between innocent childhood and commercialism shortly.

First, let's examine what it means culturally for child play to be set apart from other social activities. To do this I will help myself to some philosophers' reflections on the social meaning of play. Despite their pretensions to objectivity, philosophers inevitably reproduce – albeit with greater clarity – the cultural prejudices they inherit. What we frequently find in the philosophical account is a distillation of what otherwise seems a tangled and incoherent collection of beliefs. Yet philosophers can also shed critical light upon areas of ordinary life otherwise taken for granted. The theo-ries considered here open up both of these opportunities.

French philosopher Roland Barthes emphasises play's continuity with everyday life. Lamenting that the modern toy is merely a ready made and stylised version of the things adults use, Barthes suggests that children passively absorb cultural mandates through their objects of play. For Barthes, children are shown to their proper social place through play. Their interactions with toys – which are for Barthes merely derivative objects (trains, hairdryers, baby dolls and prams, army figurines, and so on) – induct children into their future possibilities within a tightly circumscribed social context. Most concerning for Barthes, toys condition children to own, use and consume rather than to question and create. Instead of existing radically apart from adult life, toys and play are seen to bear an imitative relation to the adult world. Furthermore, play for Barthes loses its mystique – its surplus value, perhaps – because it has a use function. Through play children practise at being the adults they will later become.[21] Thus, play is a variety of work.

This understanding of play and toys as imitative of adulthood underestimates children's critical abilities and the imaginative (sometimes subversive) manner in which they play. Yet Barthes' view rings true for many, and there is considerable concern about what children do when they play and what it means for them as potential adults. Parents worry, for instance, that their daughters will develop anorexia and unhealthy gender identities if they play with Barbie dolls, or that boys who play with toy guns might grow to be especially violent. Parents and carers tend, therefore, to want to manage how, and with what, children play. Considered as a theatre for future humanity, child play is deeply ideological, reflecting the ideas and values of the adults who supervise and regulate what children do with their time. Barthes' account reveals the extent to which we attempt to correct the faults of humanity through our children. While we express concerns about social violence reflected in children's play activities, Barthes finds in child play a deficit of creativity, for which he charges his adult contemporaries.

Italian philosopher Giorgio Agamben sees the relation between play and adult activities quite differently. While the role he gives play is highly specialised and arcane (a metaphor relating to his political philosophy), it can nonetheless help us understand how the exalted social value of children is maintained through the separation of play from everyday life. For Agamben, play is a transformative practice. Through play, he argues, the child produces toys, ordinary use objects detached from the context and activities that give them their everyday meaning. By virtue of this process of detachment, play jams the social machine – denaturing those activities from which the toy first emerged. This could be interpreted to mean that the simple act of playing with Barbies or guns can open critical insight into adult practices of the objectification of women or violence (just as hearing children repeat their own words can lead a parent to critically reflect on the violence or negativity inherent in things they routinely say). Agamben suggests that, because of the critical space it opens within daily life, play can lead to social change.

A third conception of play comes from Russian literary theorist Mikhail Bakhtin, best known for his exploration of the role of carnivalesque play in Middle Ages culture.[22] This variety of play does not discriminate between adults and children, and, indeed, obscures social boundaries in general, between nobles and common folk, and church leaders and parishioners. The carnival was an occasion for ritualised insubordination, in which social hierarchies were reversed and more informal, egalitarian relations adopted through a mode of playful ridicule of convention. During the carnival the disruptive force of laughter and of play was tolerated by the powerful so that the rigid hierarchies of church and state could hold in the normal course of life. The carnival, in this sense, provided a safe outlet for dissatisfaction about oppression, as a sphere in which the practice of play – usually dangerous to the established order – was tamed and rendered harmless.

These three accounts of play help us to understand different facets of adults' anxieties and investments in child play. For Agamben and Bakhtin, as opposed to Barthes, play is not derivative of adult life, but rather gives rise to new forms of life. For Agamben, play is inherently creative, even when it apparently only mimics adult activities. Play displaces these activities, enabling them to be reinterpreted. To approach society and the law playfully in this context means to disengage words, ideas and things from their rusted on meanings so they can be redeployed to forge new social arrangements. Play must, then, be regarded as a specific type of activity with different social effects to others such as work.

Likewise, for Bakhtin (carnivalesque) play is essentially socially disruptive, rendered safe only by virtue of the ritual limits imposed upon its practise. As the carnival constrained play's unsettling effects in renaissance times, today play is relegated to the childhood sphere, which buffers the destructive consequences of play as it is already separated from the realities of everyday political life. If we search for the meaning of child play following Bakhtin's theory of the carnival, then it comes to occupy the place of an emotional outlet for adults, who vicariously flout the social order through the play of children. In turn, child play comes to be seen as dangerous as soon as it strays into the adult world and becomes real. It can then quickly turn to violence, or at least threatens to do so in the adult imagination. This is perhaps why the British case of the slaying of toddler Jamie Bulger by two preteen boys resonates so profoundly with adult fears. Play, if not kept to the abstract sphere of Action Man™ and hopscotch, can rupture into catastrophe.

As Barthes feared, play and toys sometimes exhibit the prevailing ideology of the day in a way that can magnify contradictions within a culture, but as Agamben suggests, this also lends to play a critical potential. The game of Cowboys and Indians, for instance, so deeply problematic now, may have induced a sense of discomfort in some adults of the 1950s and 1960s, as it revealed the hypocrisy of American frontier narratives. Likewise, there is a great deal of disquiet in Australia today about the games children play (for example, with Bratz dolls) and what they reveal about contemporary culture. Yet while child play produces disquiet, and perhaps a basis for social critique, it is less certain that it gives rise to actual social change. For the most part, no great insight has been generated by public discussions of how children play, and the anxiety play produces is rarely resolved by a change in the way we organise society.

Agamben's reflections are probably next to useless, then, if we want to learn something about play's potential for producing social change. Yet his account of play – and the cultural prejudices that burden it – is highly instructive of the exalted significance given to the child in contemporary society. In his essay 'In Praise of Profanation', Agamben discusses a relationship (forgotten to our secular world) between the sacred and the profane. This relationship informs our feelings about children's place in our world. Agamben defines as sacred whatever has been removed – such as the child – 'from the free use and commerce of men' and delivered to the gods through sacrifice or ritual.[23] Whatever is profane, conversely, has been returned to everyday use (such as JonBenét Ramsey, for instance, or any other child fallen into the world of work and toil). Agamben thus emphasises the cultural power of separation. An object's context, and the prohibitions regulating its use, determines its meaning and what we may do with it. The task of religion, for Agamben, is to manage the relationship between divinity and humanity so that no contamination can take place between them. For while the human would sully and defile divinity, contact with the divine might destroy what is human.

Play subverts and undermines these distinctions by mockingly mixing the profane and the sacred. For Bakhtin, too, play's power is as a critical practice in both senses of the word 'critical': as questioning and disruptive of the social order, as well as vital to cultural renewal. The significance of play, for Agamben, is that it is 'an organ of profanation'. By removing them from their proper context and stripping them of their conventional meaning, play transforms everyday objects into toys. Yet, by the same token, play also renders objects sacred by withdrawing them from ordinary use. This in fact resonates strongly with our intuitions about play: that child play is valuable because it is not determined by utility, the imperative that governs every other relationship in our secular, capitalist world. Children consecrate objects by playing with them in a culture for which innocence is the new sacred and children its high priests.

If public discourse about the sanctity of childhood sometimes resounds with a religious tonality, it is because through it the separations that organise modern life are communicated, questioned and renewed. Innocence is maintained by the separation of the sphere of childhood from the sphere of adulthood. Children are purveyors of innocence, who fulfil this task by being adorable and mischievous, but ultimately compliant. Adult fantasies of childhood are supported by the restriction of profane information (relating to adult themes) that would defile the sacred innocent. But if we believe children must be protected from such profane material, adults also require children to manage their equally defiling innocence. Like divine messengers – or angels – children mediate adults' relation to an innocence that might otherwise destroy them. An adult who was innocent in the sense that children are innocent would be worse than useless, and probably dangerous. Innocence must be relinquished in order that one might live autonomously in society.

In this way, innocent children live by virtue of their adult protectors, and by means of innocent children – kept apart in their play world – adults are allowed access to a divine aspect of existence: a value that transcends ordinary life and makes it worthwhile.

## Play as a site of exploitation: the toy as the ultimate commodity

Despite our best intentions to protect the child from the meaner aspects of life, the delineation of a separate sphere for play – apart from the everyday commerce of life – has furnished opportunities for the commercialisation of childhood. If children amuse themselves through specialised playful activities rather than alongside adult activities, they must have special equipment, goods fit to populate the magical world of childhood. Toys are in fact the ultimate commercial commodities. They are hyper real objects that have been plucked from an everyday context and rendered for pure enjoyment. They are brighter, shinier, noisier, more colourful and tactile than ordinary use objects. Toys are oversized or miniaturised, futuristic or old fashioned, as a result of which, through the toy, the child's world comes to be removed from the world of adults in both space and time, just like Alice's Wonderland.

Toys, as stylised, sensual and useless, are objects of fashion par excellence. A resistance to use in fact marks fashion: what drives fashion is a desire for the new rather than the durable. The value of the fashionable thing animated by the imperative to consume more than comfort or convenience. Remembering Marx's commodity fetish, we can see that the toy, insofar as it is fashionable, fun and playful, is the exemplary fetish object. The value of a Nintendo Wii consists in what it says about its owner – that they are cool, fun and affluent; the less we know about how it was made (and who made it) the better.

Toys are also apt accessories for the child, whose own social value, calculated apart from use or economy, inheres in their ability to embody the fetish. The child's value as fetish is an imaginary value, the outcome of two centuries of storytelling about the wonder and otherworldliness of childhood. Because childhood represents a blessed life the child is fetishised. In other words, children's cultural value is entirely dislocated from their material situation. The innocent child is thus a product of adult fantasies of escape from the demands and responsibilities of adult life. Likewise, the child's accessories – toys – must conjure a virtual world that exists apart from adult toil. The toy is an object of pure desire, indicative of absolute enjoyment. Yet if child play is supposed to remain protected from profit, labour and the demands of adult life, it is, ironically, all the more purpose built to nurture commercial interests because as a field of fantasy, the child represents to us our deepest wants and darkest fears. We feed our desires and vulnerabilities in the guise of our children's desires and frailties. Consumer therapy offers a satisfying, if temporary, salve for these emotions. The child's secluded sphere of innocence becomes a repository for all the fashionable products money can buy. Children provide a significant avenue to distinguish oneself as responsible parent and tasteful consumer. As Bourdieu shows, this is not trivial, but is integral to how contemporary citizens convey and experience their cultural and social status.

The way that consumption in relation to children satisfies adults' appetites and becomes the focus of anxiety is truly fascinating. Take, for instance, current commotions about the commercialisation of childhood in Australia. The voiced concern is that children are not only targeted by advertisers, but are also the bait advertisers dangle before a ravenous adult consumer. Paedophilic corporations thus access our wallets by provoking children's desires and, more perversely, provoke our desire with sexualised images of children. Public unease about the commercial use of children was summarised by broadcaster Philip Adams, who coined the phrase 'corporate paedophilia':

> The age of innocence? Long gone. And the corporate paedophiles move in on our kids so that they'll wear, eat, drink and play their mass-marketed products. And if the parents don't comply with the child's implanted desires, created by squillion-dollar budgets, then fracture lines can appear within the family. Parents who resist or who simply cannot afford to comply with these hammered, hypnotic demands are, all too often, seen as failing their children.[24]

Children in this scene play the part of desire itself: they are both the ultimate desiring consumers and the definitive objects of adult desire. Parents, with whom Adams urges us to identify, are left in a hopeless position, passive to the whims of their children, judgemental onlookers and commercial culture. 'We' are boxed in, incapable of delivering upon our parental mandates of providing enjoyment and protection to our children. The possibility that children are the focus of advertising or of adult desire is profoundly disturbing. At stake is the purity of childhood: the child's sanctity depends on our ability to protect them from contamination by the profanity of quotidian adult existence. Feeling is strong that those banalities through which life is maintained – work, sex, money – are improper to childhood.

Yet contemporary culture seems hell-bent not only on exposing children to them, but also rendering the child as the ideal commodity and the ideal consumer. Capitalism, which emerged within the gulf forged between adulthood and childhood (and the public and private spheres), is lately collapsing the distinction between childhood and adulthood, thereby provoking anxiety about the maintenance of the social order such distinctions support. This amounts, in the contemporary imagination, to profanation. Despite a deep-seated sense that children should be kept apart from the commercial world and its association with sex and desire, we now find children are intimately caught up in it. What I hope is becoming clear though is that children are connected to desire because of and not despite the fact they are kept apart from the sphere of exchange. It is because children are idealised as innocent, unworldly creatures that they have become the forbidden, most prized, fruit of adult desire (commercial and sexual).

This is because the highest value for consumerism is the fetish: the commodity insofar as it exceeds its use value and the material circumstances of its production. Children perfectly embody the fetish, not only because they are divorced from the mode of production (from work), but also insofar as we ignore the material circumstances of their lives and idealise them as innocents. The value of innocence consists in being apart from concrete necessities that support life in society. The ideal of innocence provides the illusion that something exists beyond the compromise and disappointment of daily life – a beyond that bestows this life with a greater meaning and purpose. Yet, tragically, to the extent that we exalt the innocent, they will be dragged back into the commerce of everyday life by our desire for innocence. Profanation in this instance is a *fait accompli* because by making a fetish of childhood innocence, we invite exploitative commercialisation, even predation, of children. The fantasy of innocent childhood is unsustainable because our very desire for it also defiles it. And we now witness, through the commercialisation of the child, the unravelling of that enchanting fantasy. No wonder we feel anxious.

## The morphing of adult and child: sexualisation of childhood

Childhood innocence depends upon the observance of a fundamental distinction between adulthood and childhood. There are behaviours, interests and appearances that seem naturally to belong to childhood, just as there are behaviours, interests and appearances that characterise adulthood. It would seem that the very fabric of our society depends on maintaining these modes of human life as distinct. But lately, discussion papers, a number of books and a deluge of media reports raise alarm that the difference between adulthood and childhood (and so the health of our society) is at risk. The basic argument is as follows.

- *Premise 1*: Children are exposed to a variety of adult material, access to which parents cannot control.
- *Premise 2*: Children are damaged by this exposure because they are developmentally incapable of processing sexual information.
- *Conclusion*: Government should regulate advertising, the whole range of products marketed to children and all forms of media they are likely to access.
- Suppressed conclusion: Panic!

To flesh out this view a little, let's look at what comedy writer, performer and founder of Kids Free 2B Kids, Julie Gale has to say.

Research shows that exposure to sexualised imagery is linked to children's experience of increased anxiety, depression, low self-esteem, body image problems, eating disorders, self harm, and sexually transmitted infections. Kids are also becoming sexually active at younger and younger ages.[25]

'Sexualised imagery' here refers to a loose omnibus of items, from billboards advertising Viagra to Bratz dolls. The claim is that exposure to anything that alludes to sex or that adults find sexy is harmful to children, and the harm is that they will become like adults: anxious, depressed and body conscious. Yet perhaps it is not information about sex *per se* that threatens our children, but unease about sexuality – modelled by parents – that produces these symptoms. Perhaps this calls for more parental engagement with what children understand about sexuality and their bodies, rather than keeping them in bubble wrap.

Another phenomenon being charted alongside the adultification of children is the infantilisation of adults. In her book *Branded*, Alissa Quart observes that while ever-younger children are targeted to identify with brands and adopt adult modes of dress, adults are also attempting to look younger by wearing styles indistinguishable from their children's. Additionally, teens and tweens set the tone for what adults regard as cool, as corporations directly solicit their opinions through focus groups and the recruitment of 'teen consultants'.[26] Children hold the cards when it comes to what's desirable, and this desire readily becomes a longing for children themselves. This effect of morphing between child and adult seems a ubiquitous feature of modern life. It worries us, because we fear what it might lead to. We reduce this fear to the figure of the paedophile, which comes to stand for a commonplace exploitation of children by commercial as well as sexual interests. This way of framing the courting of children's desire ups the ante for child protection, which would then seem to be the only available response to the corporate world's pervasive influence over our children.

We may need to step back, however, and analyse our urge to tuck children back into their protective shrouds of innocence. Children are desirable because of the place they occupy in our social imaginary as innocent. Is the appeal to a return to innocence, then, really the answer? American literary theorist James Kincaid notes that

> We see children as, among other things, sweet, innocent,
> vacant, smooth-skinned, spontaneous, and mischievous.
> We construct the desirable as, among other things, sweet,

innocent, vacant, smooth-skinned, spontaneous, and mischievous. There's more to how we see the child, and more to how we construct what is sexually desirable – but not much more. To the extent that we learn to see 'the child' and 'the erotic' as coincident, we are in trouble. So are the children.[27]

Innocence, insofar as it implies the need of protection, will always entice exploiters and marauders. The innocent is conceptualised in terms of its vulnerability, and such vulnerability is attractive within a culture that frames sexual relations in terms of conquest of the less powerful by the stronger.

The challenge with respect to the welfare of children is how to support their needs and capacities in a manner that doesn't impose upon them our desires, fears and prejudices about what it is to be a child. The concern for appropriateness of dress and behaviour – wherein what falls outside the normal sphere of childhood is deemed sexual (and dangerous) – limits the range of acceptable performances of childhood. It also risks casting out some children on the basis that they could contaminate the rest. Children who disturb preconceptions that guide adult experiences of children, namely, the notion of pure, apolitical and inexperienced childhood, often come to be demonised (see chapter 5). Not only are these children then rendered most vulnerable, but they are also the ones middle-class parents counsel their children to avoid: the weird kid who hides under his desk, the child who swears at the teacher and is always getting into trouble, the kid who hits, or talks about sex.

If we shift our focus we might see that the scandal is not so much the sexualisation of children as the infantilisation of adults who feel encumbered by others' demands and the dangers of modern life (including sexuality). Our notion of citizenship is currently transforming. We are becoming clients of our governments, whose chief function is to protect us from terror, sickness and financial ruin. The claim to citizenship in the Western state is increasingly a claim to innocence.

## The infantilisation of adulthood

Infantilisation is a cultural process that has ridden the slipstream of the idolisation of childhood innocence: the protection accorded to children is generalised. Infantilisation is the last passive vestige of a human rights doctrine that once emphasised equality of political participation. Its primary manifestation is a delicate public who feels assaulted by the pleasures and opinions of others and desires only to be ensconced in a cushion of wholesome, regularised (commodity) enjoyment. Manifestations of infantilisation abound: in patterns of consumption and recreation, in government policy responses to financial downturns and in litigation. My attention was first drawn to it after the terrorist attacks against the United States in 2001.

The moral premium given to innocence at that time was patent in the way governments and the media framed the status of Western citizens, and not only the direct victims of the attacks. This innocence warranted further violence against populations hastily associated with the perpetrators, peoples who, because they are not generally protected from harm, had relinquished their claim to innocence. As these events unfolded, what became clear was the extent to which innocence refers to one's wealth and privileged social status: to those whose economies can afford to protect them and who are not regularly ravaged by violence or poverty. In this instance, a perceived moral immunity to harm characterises the innocent rather than the virtue of having done no harm to others.

On the basis of this moral privilege, citizens relinquish responsibility for their own state of happiness or success, and for the society that provides the context in which life takes its particular shape. The upshot of the myth of childhood innocence – and the negative evaluation of political society that it entails – is that we desire to live as the child we fantasise. But such a life of ease is impossible, even for children. The result of this abrogation of responsibility in the name of innocence is the corrosion of civil society. As political philosopher Hannah Arendt provocatively argued not long after the conclusion of the Second World War, the order of value between the public and private spheres is currently reversed, so we are increasingly confused about the meaning and purpose of civic culture.

According to Arendt, at the time of the ancient Greeks, the private, familial sphere was associated with life's necessities, the provision of basic needs. By contrast, the public, political sphere was a space of freedom. In this time of the origins of democracy, freedom referred to the ability to communicate ideas and formulate positions about what constitutes the good. (Plato's *Republic* is an example of the kind of discourse that characterised this freedom.) The *raison d'être* of human life was the political life. Individual pleasure was precisely not political, belonging instead to the home (the *oikos*, or economy), the realm of necessity, nourishment, procreation and affection. Yet since the rise of liberalism after Hobbes and Locke, Arendt argues, freedom is aligned with the pleasures of the domicile, and life in the public sphere serves the private life, a life of bodily need and comfort. This life is today sentimentally represented by the figure of the child.

There are many questions Arendt's account of democracy cannot answer – about the home as a political space, for instance; in the next chapter we will reflect in more complex ways on the thoughts of Arendt, Locke and Hobbes. For the moment, it is worth noting that, in the context of the recent global economic downturn, the perversity of our attraction to innocence, and the concomitant erosion of citizenship, is acute. Citizenship, understood as the pursuit of happiness, has come lately to express itself almost solely in terms of consumption. We produce so we can consume, and we find our meaning and purpose as citizens in the consumption of goods.[28] This is what is meant by governments' call to citizens to support the flailing economy, not by producing, but by increasing consumption and debt. By buying more houses, renovating and lining our nests with expensive consumer products, we perform good citizenship. (Add two or three children to this formula, and we have the basis of a stable economy.)

## W(h)ither political agency?

At the point where private pleasures and personal safety are valued more highly than public debate and democratic participation, the prospects for political society are grim. If we want to enjoy the advantages of innocent children, we are also discovering the obstacles to autonomy and personal agency experienced by children because of their innocence. In the years since September 2001, Western governments have expressed a concern for the protection of their very important citizens. In the name of that protection, they have restricted civil freedoms and the flow of information. Laws have been written to address the new and urgent (yet nebulous) dangers we supposedly now face. The citizen who travels overseas, uses the internet or commutes by public transport is continually reminded that their lives and freedoms are under threat. We are reassured that our government is ever vigilant, and we need not worry enough to stop shopping. Don't ask about specific dangers: the government will tell you on a need-to-know basis. And don't complain either: you're lucky to be here. Your government loves and cares for you. Doesn't that make you something like a child?

Such restriction of knowledge and heightening of fear cripples political agency: the ability to live one's life freely and affect change where it is needed, to have an impact on the world outside one's own newly renovated livingroom. If we are to take back the responsibilities of citizenship, we may need to rethink our conception of society and the place of children within it. The child currently plays the part of whatever exists outside society, where citizens locate their freedoms. This mythical outside is the imaginary repository for all that is excluded by political life: sensual pleasure, emotion and nourishment, as well as savagery. Innocence glosses these diverse experiences and affects, but at its most minimal it refers to one who has not yet entered society because they are not yet contaminated by knowledge or experience. As long as we understand the child in this way, children will not be able to exercise agency with respect to their own lives, or influence the life of the community. More than this, while the child plays this role in our cultural mythology, the possibility that all citizens may be identified as innocents or savages, rendered outside the political system and outside the rights of man is ever-present.

In chapter 3, the meaning of the child for political philosophy, and of the home for political renewal will be considered.

# Chapter 3

# The communal fantasy and its discontents

## The child's place in political community

> *Tonight, in our rich and beautiful country, there are children living out a Hobbesian nightmare of violence, abuse and neglect.*

Thus former Prime Minister John Howard begins a speech giving his reasons for a military-style federal intervention into Northern Territory Aboriginal communities.[1] The Northern Territory intervention involved the deployment of medical teams, social workers, police and army personnel on a scale unprecedented on Australian soil. It was – and, for Aboriginal peoples, continues to be – a grand assertion of state rule, a claim of legitimacy built on the ability to protect its citizens from savagery. Howard was able to initiate this audacious action – with the support of the Labor Opposition – because the central focus of his plea was the welfare of innocent children (see chapter 5 for further discussion).

The concern of the present chapter is the influence of a history of Western political thought upon how we understand political community and identity, and in turn, on the kinds of policy decisions and value judgements made today with respect to children. The prime minister no doubt had very practical reasons (not solely related to child welfare) for intervening in Northern Territory communities. Yet, curiously, his first port of call when justifying this decision was a 17th century philosopher, Thomas Hobbes. What proportion of the Australian public could Howard expect were *au fait* with the finer points of Hobbes' social contract theory? The thing is they didn't need to be. Hobbes' ideas about the 'nasty, brutish' brevity of life without law and order have infiltrated our cultural imagination. Awareness of the twists and turns of Hobbes' philosophical argument is immaterial to the rhetorical power exercised by the idea of a Hobbesian nightmare. These ideas have, for centuries, informed a European sensibility about how we should live and how we should relate to others.

Howard's framing of the prospects of Australian Aborigines in terms of the Hobbesian scenario motivated strong public sentiment against them, principally, fear. The fear instilled by Howard's state of nature was on behalf of children. Such a fear was not difficult to inspire, because we are all so attuned to the melancholy chord struck by the combination of the words 'child', 'threat' and 'fear.' This chapter will explore the extent to which children are at once central to and marginalised by the processes through which we define ourselves: in our lived interactions and in theoretical formulations of who we are. The innocent child is in fact a by-product of the productive individual or citizen constructed within modern political thought, a precious pearl that forms from the intense emotional grit deposited within the private sphere.

Because the notion of childhood plays such an important role in orienting Western identity, children are protected but also feared, posed as society's problem or ambiguously ignored within discourses of political theory. This is because children are viewed at best as incomplete and incompetent political actors, at worst as remnants of an animalistic past that threatens the ordered life of the *polis*. Children are associated with a state of nature within the political order, and for this reason, they are also viewed as society's internal danger. Yet children are also potential citizens, and so must be incorporated into society if, at some future time, they are to take up the mantle of citizenship with competency. It is the management of this process of incorporation – the transition from innocent brute to capable citizen – that gives grand political theories unease. Accounts of protopolitical childhood, such as Jean-Jacques Rousseau's *Émile* (to which I will turn later), attempt to resolve this discomfort.

Meanwhile, in the normal course of life, children receive the negative residues of these apparently abstract deliberations on political subjectivity. The entire contradictory compendium of thoughts and emotions arising from our notions of what uncivilised humanity might look like are projected onto the child. At once barbaric and innocent, unpredictable and natural, the child represents for political theory a prehistoric past, the future that must be saved and a problem to be solved. This charter extends into the way that politics is conducted every day.

The previous chapter left us with the future of childhood in crisis and sentiments towards children acutely incongruent. We also saw that this bears upon experiences of citizenship through an infantilisation of adulthood. Let's trace this situation back to one of its roots in political philosophy: the birth of the modern political subject.

## Who broke the social contract? The making and unmaking of political subjectivity

Where do our expectations about what makes a good citizen come from? What should we expect of our government? What are essential properties of civilised humanity? What are its limits? What does it mean to belong to a political community?

Most people have strong views about these issues, although their views are sometimes inconsistent and often mediated by other concerns, such as their rights as taxpayers or as parents, the civility (or incivility) of others towards them, or who does or does not belong within the scope of our concern. Living in a community means having to get along with strangers. It means having to tolerate a variety of behaviours and attitudes that sometimes challenge one's own values. It also means having to exercise restraint regarding things you might like to do – from nose picking in public to charging to the front of the coffee queue. There are things people generally refrain from doing for the sake of social harmony. These small, daily compromises typify civil life, which is an ongoing negotiation between the good of the individual and that of the community. Sometimes compromise seems too difficult and outbursts take place, leaving in their wake a sense that the social fabric has been damaged. The Cronulla race riots, for instance, represented a brutal incursion against ideals of civil, multicultural Australia for some (while for others they served to demonstrate the limit of what it means to be Australian). Much is at stake in these vaguely articulated notions of social identity, as eruptions such as that in Cronulla, which are rare in Australia, demonstrate.

While the race riot provides a sharp indication of what would happen were we to cease behaving civilly, children figure as a daily counterpoint to ideals of citizenship. Children occupy a paradoxical role in relation to the creation and maintenance of civil identity because the idea of the child furnishes both a contrast against which to define good citizenship, and an ideal that, through good citizenship, we protect. Children are disciplined and indulged precisely because they are not yet fully socialised, not yet capable of putting aside their immediate desires in order to act appropriately. On one hand, responsible parenting involves preparing children for the demands they will take up in adulthood. It is also recognised that the state will provide infrastructure (in the form of schooling) to assist children to learn how to live with others. There are also settings in which children are not tolerated because of their lack of social finesse, venues intended as retreats from social stress, such as a day spa, an up market restaurant, or locations of heightened stress, such as the workplace or funerals. On the other hand, we treasure children because of their social naivety. There is something refreshing about their inappropriateness or their failure to conform to social norms. Children's *faux pas* are often the humorous subject of parents' conversations. A benign gaff, if uttered by a child, is charming, whereas from an adult it would be absurd. Through their myriad inappropriate gestures, children's innocence is celebrated.

But we also enjoy a sense of relief in children's inadequateness because we continue to rehearse our own social roles – our own appropriateness – in relation to them. In other words, adults see their own inappropriateness reflected in children's behaviour, and so distract attention to them: 'Look at the silly child. How cute! (I'm glad nobody caught *me* doing that).' Being a citizen is not something that is accomplished once and for all. Rather, we refine our social being on an ongoing basis. Children are held responsible for adults' sense of inadequacy or failure to properly play a role. We focus on these inadequacies in the child so as to avoid confronting the inconsistency of our own social identities. The child's role in political society is therefore complex, and subject to the vicissitudes of adult modes of sociability. This equivocal status is reflected in philosophical accounts of political subjectivity or the experience of being subject to politics.

The story of modern political subjectivity begins with the theory of social contract, and it is in relation to this contract that children are consigned the place of the citizen's excess, both unruly and innocent.

## The social contract and the citizen's identity

Social contract theory, through the social contract scenario, narrates how citizens are able to have standing in relation to the state. At the beginning of modernity, it marks a new manner of thinking about this relationship. Prior to about the 17th century, individuals were subjects of the realm, and kings held power through divine right. In proposing a story of the origins of political society, philosophers such as Hobbes, Locke and Rousseau brought into play the idea that the human being, regardless of social rank, is imbued with natural rights and freedoms. We could then imagine an individual to whom the state is accountable, and whose obedience depends on the recognition of inalienable rights (security and the enjoyment of private property, for instance). The social contract negotiates a transition, then, between primitive, natural rights-bearing humanity and the citizen with obligations to the body politic. The contract means that as individuals we temper our rights so we can live together. While in the state of nature we act in our own interests; in political society we acquire a sense of shared interests and goals and of a civic duty to act in accordance with them. Political subjectivity, then, has two registers:

1  we must act in accordance with the values of the community
2  we must believe in these values and make them our own.

Personal identity is connected to communal identity: we know who we are in relation to those to whom we have responsibilities.

The natural individual is, in turn, not entirely overcome, but persists within the *polis* to check the powers of the state. We must moderate selfish desires for the good of the community, but the rights reserved for the individual limit such compromise. Political life in liberal society attempts to balance individual and collective welfare; state institutions are supposed to manage these competing interests. The social contract philosophers dramatise such tensions, each interpreting a little differently the relation between the individual and political community. As we saw in the quotation cited by Howard, Hobbes' picture of life before the social contract is bleak. Writing during England's civil war, Hobbes emphasised the need for stability. Nature's freedoms produce brutal competition, resolvable only by a strong ruler. Hobbes' political community, then, is weighted in the state's favour, and freedom of expression verges too near to insurrection for his comfort.

Locke, conversely, favours what we today call small government. A precursor to liberalism, Locke saw the state's concern not in determining the values of its citizens, but rather in providing a framework for the neutral arbitration of disputes. The social contract leaves natural humanity relatively unaltered, even augmenting its freedom with supporting legal institutions. Similarly, Rousseau favours natural man over society, and the state fosters the virtues of nature in citizens through educational and democratic institutions. For Rousseau, as for Locke, the goal of the social contract is the preservation of our natural freedom. However, for Rousseau, the citizen's task is onerous because society corrupts. He argues that in nature the solitary individual is taught by direct experience. 'He' is continuous with nature, thus understanding the limits of his desire. Conversely, in society, each wants what belongs to his neighbour, and trusts books and authority rather than experience. This leads to the perversion of nature, or what for Rousseau amounts to the same thing: inequality, greed and injustice. Citizenship, as opposed to subjection, involves carefully guarding one's inner nature against others' excessive desires. But it also involves the ability to adjust one's desires to the general will, or the will of a majority of other citizens who have likewise cultivated their inner nature.

From Hobbes' first foray into the idea of prepolitical man to its adaptation at the hands of Locke and Rousseau, the limits between the state and natural man eroded. Hobbes had sought to protect humanity from itself. He saw natural man as fallen, bereft of God and in need of the sovereign's authority. Locke and Rousseau, to the contrary, were optimistic about human nature. Each sought to include natural man within politics, so that it was regulated and protected. The firm difference Hobbes established between before and after the political community is minimised by these later philosophers. Non-political (natural) life is incorporated within the *polis* as the family, and the rights and freedoms that limit the state's power.

Even within the self, the boundary between natural and civilised humanity remains porous and ill defined. The social contract is presented as if it were a moment in historical time at which we all came together and decided to constitute a community. This event is presumed to have had a transformative effect upon individuals, who left behind their natural ways to constitute themselves as citizens. Once signed, the contract is supposed to have delivered us to a culture that enshrined our natural rights while also ensuring regularity and safety through law. In truth, the social contract is a political myth that organises our social reality, a fantasy we draw on whenever we encounter uncivilised humanity within ourselves or in others. The contract is not a moment of past time, but an ever-present juncture within political life that produces us as citizens. We can understand how the social contract works upon us in terms of what French philosopher Louis Althusser called 'hailing' or 'interpellation'.

Interpellation describes how we assume ideological truths and roles: the values and ideas that keep the social order ticking over. For Althusser, ideology does not refer simply to abstract ideas. Ideology is the material existence of ideas in our practices and relationships. Ideology is how we imagine our worldly relations insofar as they are meaningful and purposeful. Ideology explains how relations to production are reproduced: how, that is, one person knows he is a shopfitter, while another knows she is an academic, and each behave accordingly. Ideology, then, encompasses the ideals, knowledges, institutions and practices through which we learn our place. But importantly, ideology is lived. It is not only a view to which one subscribes or a set of beliefs one might transcend to reveal an underlying truth. Ideology exists within a way of life. When we go to church or a football game, cycle to work or buy a lottery ticket, ideology makes sense of these behaviours.

It is at the level of ideology that philosophy is produced, as philosophers formulate systems of thought to explain or justify social norms. Philosophers such as Hobbes, Locke and Rousseau deliver us our ideological prejudices and assumptions in a seemingly objective, incontrovertible form. They purport to reveal the reason behind action and belief, as if such reason is causally primary. In turn, actions and beliefs seem natural only because they are already steeped in ideology. Our routine practices feel reassuring because they produce us as we think we already are. Philosophy, ideology and action, then, mutually reinforce one another, delivering an apparently unassailable system of values and a true way of life. Yet ideology also provides philosophers a point of access to intervene, to become a tool of social critique. Philosophy can question the naturalness and rationality of beliefs and behaviours. Then new ways of seeing and living might become possible.

Althusser's philosophical intervention is to show how ideology confers a deeply felt individual identity through interpellation. For Althusser, people acquire a social identity through material relationships with others. He stages this idea with the example of a man halted in the street upon hearing a policeman yell 'Hey, you there!' No sooner has the man turned around, Althusser writes, than he becomes subject to the policeman's hail. His subjectivity is activated in response to the law's address. The hail of the policeman picks him out, and in this moment he becomes who he already was (a citizen who, at any time, might be called upon by the state).

There are more current and local instances that exemplify what is meant by interpellation.

- The recorded message at the train station that asks each of us to alert staff to unattended baggage, thus informing us that we are (always already) subject to an age of terror.
- The World Vision advertisement that tells us (as affluent first world citizens) that for only $1 a day we could save the life of this specific (third world) child, who beseeches us from our television screen to help them.
- The current affairs program voiceover that tells us that this is a story that no parent can afford to miss (thus investing us with the role of caring and protective parent of helpless and vulnerable children).

Each provides a meaning-giving social context together with one's specific role in relation to it. We are thereby acutely reminded of our social identity and obligations in a way that is both impersonal and intimate.

These instances not only remind us of our identity: they also incite identity by setting in play the social coordinates through which identity is enacted. 'I' am called to each of these ways of being – vigilant watcher against terrorism, affluent citizen of the first world, parent – which captures me while also producing an excess. For 'I' am more than these insufficient identities through which 'I' am realised at any given moment. This excess – the 'I' that cannot be reduced to a particular social role – is ready for a new interpellation, for every situation that should arise in one's ideological field. This excess makes identity feel like a choice, that there is someone behind the roles we play, an actor behind the act.

This excess of the social role is experienced as the real self, the locus of freedom. Remember, though, that this real self is an effect of interpellation, splitting the subject between a socially prescribed role and whatever it excludes. The excluded self appears to resist social identity, but instead provides it with a motive force, a reserve of emotional energy invested into the faithful portrayal of a role. Without this excess the political subject would be little more than a machine: we would exhaust ourselves in the fulfilment of our social roles. This possibility is what makes George Orwell's *1984* so chilling; here the demand for absolute compliance leaves no room for resistance or individuality. But while the excess of interpellation provides a sense of choice (and so a potential for deviation or dis-obedience) it also produces the anxious commitment to ideology that keeps most of us in line. Well-honed ideologies such as liber-alism manage this excess. Liberalism is synonymous with choice, and liberal subjects obey the imperatives to be free and enjoy. We invest the excess in consumer choice, through which we experience our individuality.

Like the sundry hails to subjectivity considered above, the social contract is also what Althusser calls an 'apparatus of interpellation'.

The idea of an original agreement that grounds the political community, bids the individual to put aside egotistic desires to adopt the role of citizen. The social contract hails the citizen not only in works of philosophy but also in legal judgements and the news media: criminals are punished, shoddy repairmen pursued, on the basis that there is an implicit standard of behaviour to which we all mutually agree simply by virtue of living in a community. This idea puts us in a material relation to the needs and expectations of others, and thereby produces the citizen, the one who cultivates their desires so as to act in the interests of the whole. The transition from natural individual to citizen-subject is achieved by dint of the network of social relations within which we are situated.

Yet as Althusser also points out, we imagine this transition back to front. We do not begin with an individual who is then socialised to produce the citizen. Rather, he writes,

> ideology has always-already interpellated individuals as subjects ... *individuals are always-already subjects*. Hence individuals are 'abstract' with respect to the subjects which they always-already are.[2]

Put simply, there is no individual born outside of community, as the social contract myth suggests. One already has an identity in relation to the rest. This, Althusser makes clear, is the case even for a newborn baby, who is interpellated according to social indices such as legitimacy of parentage, race, class and sex. The individual with equal rights and freedoms is a purified ideal, proposed in abstraction from the people in society, always-already subjected by the material conditions (privileged or otherwise) in which they find themselves.

What this means is that the natural individual, who supposedly precedes the hailing action of the social contract, is but a fantasy, a figment of a collective dreaming retold through narratives of political philosophy. Social contract theory gives a commonsense account of what it is to be a political subject. But the phenomena it describes are not natural; rather, they are ideologically produced. Hobbes, Locke and Rousseau encapsulated a certain understanding of human being. This fantasy is not simply an escapist indulgence, but rather shapes the political sphere. Far from an empty gesture of resistance to subjection, the idea of a coherent person who undergoes socialisation – choosing to accept or defy this process – plays a role in social subjection. The individual – the excess produced by our compliance to the social role – provides the quantum of enjoyment that emotionally and psychologically binds us to such roles. Subjection to the political community is a circular process. The individual is the fantasy of freedom from society that emerges after ideological subjection. Yet it is portrayed as having come before subjection, as the citizen's free choice that legitimates the state's authority over us. In this light, we can see that the social contract performatively reveals itself, according to the 20th century British philosopher John L. Austin's notion of the 'performative utterance', a speech act that does what it describes at the moment it is spoken (when the priest says 'I pronounce you man and wife', for instance).[3] And so, to recount the social contract means to be hailed by (and so consent to) it. The idea that at some point we had a choice produces an illusory instant of freedom within subjection, a position from which to bargain and a life independent of the social formations that structure human identity and desire.

Crucially, the freedom that binds us to subjection is imagined as outside rather than within politics. The free individual of social contract theory is a compensatory fantasy. What it compensates is our subjection to the common interest. The desire for a life lived outside such subjection produces the fantasy of natural man, which influences our regard for children and people of other cultures (whom we imagine have access to the pure enjoyment we have lost). This illusion that freedom belongs to prepolitical individuals rather than political subjects leads to the infantilisation of citizenship addressed in chapter 2. Through the notion of the individual we aspire towards independence from community. In search of the freedom natural man promises, we retreat to a sphere of intimacy in which we are permitted to indulge private pleasures. For Locke, this amounts to the pursuit of a happiness that is beyond the state's purview;

for Rousseau, the intimate sphere shields us from the distorting influence of society and keeps us connected to our true selves. From a different point of view, this retreat to the private sphere does not contribute to freedom, but rather separates us from the conditions that support freedom and agency, what Arendt called 'world', or the intersubjective plurality of views through which human uniqueness is expressed and nurtured.

Against Locke and Rousseau, Arendt laments the ascendancy of intimacy and the modern notion that the true self can be expressed only in private. In the capitalist age, the development of the sphere of intimacy, along with an emphasis on wealth and accumulation, has given rise to styles of life that isolate people from one another. In search of freedom, enjoyment and self-expression, what we find is consumption. Hobbies and leisure replace work, a more subversive (Bakhtian) mode of play, and dialogue as means of self-discovery. Community, for Arendt, represents the beginning of freedom rather than its compromise. The fantasy of natural man, before political community, is thus part of a more general cultural assault on democracy.

Given the decisive place of the individual within contemporary democratic traditions, indeed, as a catalyst for such traditions, this seems especially ironic. Yet what we take to be at stake for democracy is a way of life that privileges freedom from government intervention rather than the capacity-building freedom that requires others' support. The freedom imagined in modern democracies is modelled on the imagined freedoms of natural man, freedoms and enjoyments of an abstract individual, devoid of the social obligations and infrastructure that frame political life. Arguably, the freedom of contemporary liberal subjects Arendt spurns is a paltry enjoyment, an avoidance of pain that verges on boredom. Watching television, eating out, gambling, surfing the internet. These entertainments are but poor substitutes for a more original enjoyment we imagine children to own, a fantasised *je ne sais quoi* to which we lost access the moment we took up a social role. This lost enjoyment is innocence, but it is also something dangerous, something that threatens to rupture identity and social cohesion.

Indeed, original enjoyment signals whatever must be suppressed so that society can function. The bearers of such enjoyment are natural in that they cannot become social, and so are a menace to the *polis*. For Hobbes, the citizen's excess is the violence, selfishness and intemperance that must be subordinated at pain of death by the sovereign. For Locke, it is laziness instead of industriousness: the Native American, for instance, who, according to Locke, failed to work the land, and thereby failed to forge a claim on it. For Rousseau this dangerous excess is subtler still, comprising a weakness inherent to the innocence he so venerated: vulnerability to corruption. However we imagine this dangerous yet desirable pleasure, it is an excess that is both constructed and marginalised as soon as we are hailed to take up a social role. The excess is the intense and bewildering emotional material thrown into a distant yonder at that continually recurring moment of social interpellation.

The fantasy of the innocent child is entertained so that adults can maintain a connection to the innocence we all lost as the price of political agency. In an adult fantasy through which we relay a story about the origins of society, childhood is a resource for the political imagination and a place in which dangerous desires and emotions (such as resentment, selfishness or spontaneity) are repressed. Because these repressed, excessive elements of self are both threatening and desirable, they give rise to ambivalent attitudes towards children. Let's now explore this ambivalent excess of social identity and its effects upon those whom it marginalises.

## The child's burden and the citizen's excess

For some, such as Hobbes, natural humanity represents the verge of social collapse – like a monster drawn on an old map to signify the limit of geographical knowledge. To legitimise the Northern Territory intervention, for instance, John Howard deployed natural man as a menace to the Australian way of life. For others, natural humanity represents ideals of honest industriousness (Locke) or a Romantic goodness (Rousseau), which are themselves threatened by society and so should be protected by the state. However, both views advocate at least a partial exclusion of natural man to produce the ideal citizen. These later social contract theorists value natural man, but still take for granted that human nature must be tempered and guided through the process of civilisation. What's called natural man contains the potentialities that will give rise to political man. It is the raw material of civilisation. But the state of nature also becomes a place of containment for whatever is withheld from political subjectivity, whatever would work against the possibility of community.

Social contract theory discloses a particular way of seeing human nature, as do systems of regulation or law. Laws, and the bodies of knowledge that support them, produce us as political subjects. Yet this political subject has very particular social contours. They are male, white, propertied and free to make contracts, to bargain with their liberty. These laws and knowledges also produce an excluded remainder that is thought to exist outside or before politics: Indigenous peoples, whose relation to the land does not reflect Locke's system of possession and alienation, criminal and 'insane' people, administered by legal and health systems, women, traditionally confined to the home and, finally, children, who must be educated and managed to adulthood. Members of these groups bear the burden of our philosophical prejudices: they are the remnants of citizenship. Children and tribal peoples, in particular, provide ideological fancies with a material outlet, as we place them on a dubious timeline, the apex of which is the contemporary adult of European extraction. So-called primitive ways of life form the basis of imagining our cultural past. White Australia in particular constructs its ideal of citizenship through a complex relation to tribal people by means of what Sigmund Freud called 'projection'.

Projection is a psychological response to facets of the self at odds with the ideal self, and from which we therefore wish to distance ourselves. We project these inconvenient traits onto another, who then stands in for our unwanted, excess self. This Other is invariably perceived as antisocial or embarrassing, and we punish them for it. At the community level underprivileged groups such as, but not only, single mothers and cultural minorities, often play this part, attracting a violence of emotion that is patently irrational. Over-privileged celebrities such as Britney Spears, Amy Winehouse and NRL warriors, are also frequently figures of derision, through which ordinary people take up an attitude to their own moments of overindulgence. It's easier to manage anxiety about our own excesses if we conflate them with the faults of others, which enables us to encounter disowned aspects of the self in safety. Through psychological projection, we are able to transform anguish about ourselves into enjoyment of cruelty towards another.

The problematic relationship of European Australians to the people we displaced can be understood in these terms. By viewing Australian Aborigines as a less developed people, non-Indigenous Australians have refused to recognise their specificity: that their trajectory has been different from ours because the material conditions that shape their societies are unique. This amounts to a refusal to respect their autonomy from European Australians. Colonials happened upon Aborigines as if upon an image of themselves in a fairground mirror. Only by imagining away others' difference and autonomy can we project upon them the obverse side of our own identities. Because white Australia needs to work through its own savagery, Indigenous peoples appear savage to them. Native peoples are thus parodied as irrational, emotional, drunken and underdeveloped, so as to shore up white Australians' self-image as rational, intelligent, sober and civilised. Thus is the work of projection: the self maintains its goodness by identifying all contradictory evidence with another. By the same token, when others' difference is erased, the good values accruing to the self also bleed into them. Hence the more positive and idealised associations with tribal peoples: that they are happy, simple, noble and pure of heart. The coloniser finds these traits when he looks for his origins in the colonised Other. Insofar as this Other is an extension of the self, they will be tainted by the mixed emotions through which self-esteem is negotiated.

The porous relation between the coloniser and colonised can be mapped onto the social contract allegory. Whiteness, when viewed as the culmination of a process of civilisation, is a transformed and refined version of blackness, which must pass through a distinctly European apparatus of interpellation (the social contract) to become fully human. It is only once Indigenous people are interpreted as the raw material of a more mature mode of being human that they can also be understood as failures of civilisation – or the white man's burden.[4] And in this way they serve perfectly, yet ironically, as a surface for the projection of our own failure to be civilised.

Similarly, as colonisation positions Indigenous peoples at the beginning of a timeline leading inevitably to modern European subjectivity, children also serve fantasies about our personal prehistories. Childhood represents an innocent past we nostalgically recall as simpler and more complete. Accordingly, we project onto children the resentments we feel about our own process of maturation, and longing for the ease of life without responsibility. The relation between adults and children is ambivalent insofar as we are attached to our socialisation but also feel damaged by it. We appreciate the accoutrements of civilisation, the value-added fruit of surplus labour made possible by the social contract. All that theoretically makes us human – from science to literature and the arts – are benefits of post-contract life. Yet we also feel separated from an inner, more primordial, self through this process. The fantasy of the innocent child – apart from the rest of society – represents an attempt to recuperate this primordial self. Children then become the adult's burden, envied as an innocent, savage simplicity, projected onto them from the remnants of self the citizen must reject.

The relationship between children (as adults' burden) and tribal peoples (as white man's burden) is not incidental. Children are labelled savages as easily as Aborigines are labelled children ('Your new-caught sullen peoples, Half devil and half child', in the words of Rudyard Kipling). The connection between actually existing individuals and a hypothetical, prepolitical way of being is redoubled through the use of these cross-referenced jeers. The marginalisation that results from the notion that children and Indigenous peoples are outside the political sphere is debilitating to the agency available to these groups. They are caught up with one another in a lawless space of freedom, before the social contract gathered citizens in political community. But what could freedom be without laws or politics? For children no less than adults are subject to a social position and tied to social obligation. They have, in addition, to bear the enormous burden of our fantasies of innocence and freedom. How, then, did innocence become a political prison for children? How did children come to be held hostage to Western philosophy's misguided conception of freedom?

As Althusser points out, how political systems reproduce themselves through subjects' inner experience is a question that nags political theory. For canonical political philosophers such as Rousseau and Locke this question was central to producing good citizens and democratic institutions. In texts of political philosophy, the child is positioned as the raw material invested with the citizen's desire and identity. Anxiety about the reproduction of ideology is connected to the child, who is for political philosophy both an insoluble problem and its enigmatic answer. While Locke approached the question of political subjectivity through an analysis of human understanding that situates the child as a blank slate (*tabula rasa*), Rousseau, while claiming to follow the path of nature, developed a strict regime of education that leaves nothing to chance. Accordingly, the child is cast as an unruly yet vital element of our political future. Children are the volatile substance of politics that must be controlled and carefully handled, lest humanity lose its way.

Children are viewed as possessing the original freedom we all want, and for this reason are feared, controlled and protected, worried about and, ultimately, blamed.

## Only a child can save us: the figure of the child in philosophy

The modern idea of the child – as innocent, and for this reason valuable – was formalised and given momentum in the liberal thought of John Locke. This idea developed in the context of competition between notions of what it is to be human. The terrain of childhood, in this context, emerged as representative of humanity in its purest and starkest forms.

The view of humanity current in Locke's time derived from biblical interpretation, particularly Saint Augustine's theory of original sin, whereby each of us embodies the fall. Because Adam and Eve disobeyed and were cast out of paradise, humanity, it was thought, had lost its way. From the moment we are born into this accursed world, according to Augustine, we continue to grow farther from God's divine perfection. Piety consists of recognising our infinite debt to God and, through careful devotion, bringing our will into alignment with His. Hobbes epitomises this view of humanity. His state of nature does not represent an original humanity in the Garden of Eden, but rather life after the fall. Natural man depicts a humanity that severed its connection to a truth previously available through obedience to God's authority. Hobbes's sovereign takes the place of this divine source of truth, thus fixing an order of value that otherwise would remain up for grabs.

According to this view, children are prone to impiety and in need of firm authority. William Golding's classic novel, *Lord of the Flies*, a staple of the Australian secondary school syllabus, exemplifies this outlook. A group of schoolboys becomes marooned on a desert island; there are no adult survivors. These well-educated English boys rapidly descend into savagery, showing that without adult supervision children are drawn to anarchy and cruelty. The children on Golding's island represent a microcosm of the adult world, which is also fallen and in need of a stern hand. This literary device is not unusual: children are repeatedly brought into play to conceptually distil humanity's nature.

Locke opposed this view of humanity, which he believed to be essentially good. He recommended that children, as the purest exemplars of humanity, should be given bibles especially tailored to their needs, with the seedier and more violent aspects excised.[5] Locke's new notion of childhood also served his nascent epistemology, or theory of knowledge, in particular, his contention that knowledge is formed through a sensible relation to the world instead of inborn. Rationalists such as Descartes had argued that true knowledge originates from communion with the soul, accessed intuitively. For Descartes contemplative withdrawal from the sensual world brings knowledge. For Locke, conversely, knowledge is derived only from experience. Whereas Augustine overburdens humanity with original sin and Descartes congests the mind with innate ideas, Locke sees the human being and the mind as originally empty of content: *tabula rasa*. According to Locke's empiricism, events impress themselves onto the mind to shape how we encounter new information. After many repetitions of the same phenomenon (for example, the sun rising from the east) we can generalise from experience. We develop the capacity to predict and understand from lived experience, not because of a knowledge installed within us by God. We are born innocent of knowledge but with the capacity to organise sensation, to construct knowledge piece by piece.

Locke's child is thus an apt synecdoche for humanity, a part representing the whole in its essence as pure and untainted by inscrutable, unworldly truths. In line with the newness and simplicity of his account of knowledge, Locke's view of humanity is reflected in the child. The new subject of knowledge and politics is an intrepid explorer of his world, a scientific investigator free of the weight of millennia of superstition and ignorance. He is a clean slate, ready to write himself as the truth of the cosmos. But more than this, the child is for Locke humanity's *tabula rasa*, signifying the point from which we can start anew, with a hope for a better future. Above all, Locke sketches a human-centred universe such that humanity is on the ascendancy rather than the unworthy progeny of a fall. For the first time the idea that children are innocent can take a definitive hold on the collective imagination, principally because humanity now understands itself as essentially innocent.

This understanding of innocence as a freshness of perspective and humanity's new dawn is further romanticised by Rousseau, who deploys the child in his battle against a decadent society. Following Locke's humanism, Rousseau deeply distrusted authority-based knowledge because in his view tradition gives rise to inequality. Rousseau's social contract involved a complete renegotiation of political systems, just as his educational treatise (*Émile*) recommended a course of learning that strips bare the artifices of education, bringing the student instead into a direct relation to nature. From a point of view that privileges exploration over conventional sources of information, it is understandable that the child would become the beacon for a new humanity. For Rousseau children are unburdened by superstition and nonsense, unblemished by social norms. By observing children, he claimed to have gained insight into 'the first and the truest movements of nature, about which all the most learned men know nothing'.[6] While children are the purest exemplars of humanity, they are also most vulnerable to corruption by absurd cultural practices. 'God makes all things good; man meddles with them and they become evil'. he begins Book 1 of *Émile*. For Rousseau, the problem of politics amounts to the contamination of the human spirit. Children begin life as good, so if we save the child, we save the man. Through an exacting regulation of childhood, Rousseau believes we can produce a citizen worthy of the title.

Let's pause now to reflect on this important moment in the conception of childhood as we know it today, as a privileged point of intervention to secure a better future. Following Locke's lead,[7] Rousseau departed from a tradition of regarding children as bestial, at best miniature adults and at worst miniature devils. Rousseau attributes to children their own psychological condition and form of knowledge, which, he says, it is vital we recuperate. He writes that

> We know nothing of childhood and with our mistaken
> notions the further we advance the further we go
> astray . . . The wisest writers devote themselves to what
> man ought to know, without asking what a child is capable
> of learning. They are always looking for the man in the
> child, without considering what he is before he becomes
> a man.[8]

Despite the enchantment of children, Rousseau's quest for childhood is motivated by a concern for the production of good citizens rather than a special concern for the wellbeing of children. Rousseau considers the child's nature a resource for the political community: its embryonic future, the potential citizen.

Rousseau's vision of a new childhood was consistent with his account of the state of nature. The unsocialised child was emblematic of a minimal, pure, unconscious humanity. Yet Rousseau's child also emerged in the context of a range of economic and political changes (principally, the growth of the middle classes) that brought about a re-evaluation and refinement of childhood. Rousseau successfully articulated a current already emerging within his social milieu; riding the crest of the mercantile culture that came to succeed aristocracy, he will be remembered as the founder of modern educational practice and childhood studies.

But Rousseau's legacy also extends to a way of thinking about childhood that places an enormous social burden on children. As they came to be seen as the centre of the family, and later as the *raison d'être* of society, governments began to increasingly intervene in children's lives in order to save society. Émile, the son Rousseau never raised,[9] is supposed to represent best practice in the education of the citizen by nature. (Likewise, Émile's ideal woman, Sophie, is given a simple education to prepare her not to be a citizen, but to be a complimentary – passive – mate for Émile.)[10] The insight Rousseau brought to social contract theory was that the circumstances through which political subjectivity emerges are determined within the household. In order to consider this formative aspect of citizenship, Rousseau theorised in *Émile* the domestic arrangements that would best support democracy. Rousseau gave women and children a role to play in the creation of the good society, and saw a need to negotiate the citizen's emergence from the home to the political field, to defeminise the (male) citizen. In essence, he set out to show every person to their role within the family as well as the public sphere in the manner of the interpellation, which invests each with their social function. His technique is effective, if somewhat crude by today's standards: 'Tender, anxious mother, I appeal to you . . .', he addresses his women readers at the beginning of the book. Thus he picks them out in their social identity as mothers, authorising their value and stake in the republic to come.

*Émile* paved the way for the development in public discourse of a notion of the private sphere as integral to politics, a commonplace today that was still unresolved in Rousseau's time. *Émile* created a language for the minutiae of bodily existence, enabling the political cultivation and management of life. While Rousseau had rescued the child from animality (admonishing mothers for swaddling babies and hanging them from trees), he returned the child to a state of nature within political society. The family now came to be conceptualised as a biological as well as a political space, a place of reproduction of life and of ideology, rather than the economic space it had been previously. This conceptual adjustment has had lasting effects on family life. Thanks largely to the careful attention Rousseau paid to the emotional relationships that undergird nation, the child has become the chief handle of the family tool through which citizens (recast as parents) are governed. Children now embody the intimacy of the home that is supposed to complete the individual. It is in considering the child that we endeavour to build the good society. Like Rousseau's little Émile, with the aid of a good parenting manual and a good education, every precious modern day darling should become a model citizen.

But are there better ways to envisage contemporary citizenship? Do we possess the imagination for them? If we equate childhood with a freedom we believe exists only outside politics and accessible only through children, childhood is paradoxically thoroughly invested with political meaning. Equally, if children's experiences of culture and society must be mediated and controlled by even the most benevolent tutor (such as Émile's), then every accidental encroachment of an external reality – that is, a reality that is perceived to be adult – becomes politicised as a crisis. (This is especially so where money or sexuality are involved.) If, conversely, we accept that freedom is not elsewhere but is possible only within a network of social relationships and grounded in mutual dependency, then we may also conceive of children as participants in the political, not only as its objects. In agreement with Hannah Arendt, then, I would stress that responsibility, citizenship and freedom take place in an intersubjective context wherein autonomy does not mean casting others adrift (loaded up with our projected debris), but rather taking account of others' perspectives in the process of one's own emergence. We need to question the liberal notion of individualism that undergirds the experience of politics, of the natural man who freely trades away his rights for protection. Freedom and autonomy in this context imply a total lack of constraint that ignores political and familial context. Such a conception of freedom inevitably tramples others' freedoms, pitting its interests against theirs.

The contemporary influential contract philosopher John Rawls addresses these limitations of liberalism by means of a thought experiment that, I would contend, repeats its predecessors' problems. Revisiting the social contract, Rawls bids us to imagine material relations are entirely rearranged so we no longer know whether we stand in relation of privilege or subjugation to others. 'I' might be black or white, rich or poor, male or female, disabled or able bodied, young or old, without knowing either way.

> [N]o one knows his place in society, his class position or social status; nor does he know his fortune in the distribution of natural assets and abilities, his intelligence and strength, and the like.[11]

Rawls' hypothesis is that when deliberating over the fairest principles upon which to found society, this veil of ignorance would compel each to acknowledge the interests of the most vulnerable in case that place turns out to be their own. Through this thought experiment we are returned to what Rawls calls the 'original position', his analogue for natural man. It is from this socially neutered position that we create a fair society.

This experiment reveals how our interests and choices exist already in a social context: according to relationships to others of relative privilege or underprivilege. But Rawls' suggestion that it is possible to efface one's situation, as if these attributes that so deeply affect subjectivity could be shed like so many clothes, returns us to a notion of humanity and of rationality that is asocial. A faith in the natural man preceding the social contract persists in Rawls' formulation. When it comes to explaining how decision making is possible, instead of emphasising the critical importance of social relations, Rawls situates the subject within the asocial original position, and then builds from first principles a theory of rationality grounded in neutrality (or the absence of interest). This has adverse effects for children's freedom.

Children are depicted as only partially rational, or as not yet rational, and thus are excluded from the original position, denied (along with animals and mentally disabled people) a place at the table in the negotiation of a new social contract. Indeed, Rawls defines the community of rational individuals who decide the contract as 'contemporary rational adults', so as to control for difference in his negotiators' capacities and so ensure the fairest outcome. In so doing, Rawls neglects to consider that children might have specific interests and in so doing removes their opportunity to represent these interests. Indeed, by excluding those he deems insufficiently rational, Rawls weakens the egalitarian effect intended by the veil of ignorance. While I might imagine I am a child just as convincingly as I could imagine I am poor or black, if there are no actual children allowed to participate in democratic deliberation we are confined to the fantasy realm.

Tellingly, Rawls addresses children's prospects in deliberating the new society at the same moment as he signals the need to protect us 'against our own irrationality',[12] with the introduction of the principle of paternalism:

> In the original position the parties assume that in society they are rational and able to manage their own affairs . . . But once the ideal conception is chosen, they will want to insure themselves against the possibility that their powers are undeveloped and they cannot rationally advance their interests, as in the case of children . . .[13]

The principle of paternalism authorises rational parties to make decisions on behalf of the incapacitated (such as children), and so is supposed to ensure that their interests are represented. But how can this innovation reflect anything apart from values already enshrined in our culture? Isn't paternalism towards children, people with disabilities and others considered less rational (remembering that at one stage this included women and Indigenous peoples) already the *status quo*? Rawls' return to social contract theory is an attempt to eliminate injustices pervasive of contemporary society, putting in place from the beginning a fair and equitable structure for social relationships. What contract thinking misunderstands is the profoundly social and intimate nature of freedom, which flourishes in society's midst, not in abstraction from it.

As Arendt suggests, we are only able freely to emerge as who we are by dint of the intersubjective background that receives us. In contrast to Arendt, however, I would add that this process of coming into one's own could occur equally in the home as in the public sphere. As feminists have long argued, the personal is political. Rather than viewing the domicile – where so-called apolitical activities such as washing, nourishing and raising children take place – as a retreat from politics, it might be said that these intimate, familial relations are deeply political. Even so, these relations often resemble a medieval fiefdom more than a modern democracy, structured hierarchically according to age, gender and pay.

Rawls' own description of parties behind the veil of ignorance as 'heads of households'[14] illustrates this point. He assumes a paternalistic attitude will ensure that all interests are taken into account. But isn't this idea precisely what democracy questions? Isn't this what the social contract is supposed to address? If we cannot now imagine that children might have something intelligible to say about their own interests, however did Locke or Rousseau imagine adults could in relation to the state? Perhaps democracy needs to begin at home through the inclusion of children as well as their parental representatives in decisions affecting households and communities. Is it possible to imagine fora that cultivate an onus to listen to others and to accommodate their needs to one's own? As with Rawls' model, this is a deliberative situation, but grounded in a particular social context (the family) that does not exclude members deemed insufficiently rational.

Children are as capable as adults of responding to others' views if such views are offered in the spirit of reciprocity. Involvement in family and community decision making not only empowers children, but also allows them to experience the responsibility to others that attends agency and freedom. It teaches that freedom always has limits, and is both bounded and facilitated by others' interests. It is a truism that children require limits, but these limits needn't consist only of a parental no. Rather, the limits children and adults require emerge from a social context, from others' desires and the obligation to consider them. In this way, such a deliberative, democratic practice also develops adults' capacity to comprehend what freedom is and how we can live with others. This practice is more difficult but more rewarding than exercising authority over children and underestimating their capacities. Through re-imagining the possibilities for household politics and our relations with children, we are less prone to indulge projective fantasies of savages, not quite humans, and innocents in need of protection.

Chapter 4 turns to the question of how we presume to know about children's nature and capacities, within and outside the familial context.

# Chapter 4

# **Disciplining innocence**

## Knowledge, power and the contemporary child

Childhood innocence is often equated with a state of unworldly naivety considered both precarious and enviable. Western culture values this blissful ignorance in our children so much that enormous economic, emotional and rhetorical resources are invested in maintaining it, in protecting children, that is, from the kinds of knowledge and experience that make the rest of us feel world weary. Through the carefully crafted ignorance fostered in children, an enchanted world is maintained that we can occasionally glimpse through their eyes. We manipulate their environment to produce belief in paranormal creatures (hiding chocolate eggs at Easter, sprinkling fairy dust at bedtime, leaving biscuit crumbs on Christmas morning and perhaps riskiest of all, exchanging lost teeth for hard cash under their sleeping heads). But we do so innocently and for their own good. After all, children have the rest of their lives to grow sour. What harm could a belief in Santa Claus or the Easter bunny do? Why disturb their paradise?

One reason for caution about the creation of such an enchanted realm is that after paradise comes a fall. When children are polluted by what is regarded as the adult world, adults are quickly disenchanted with them. The fantasy world we build for children is in fact our paradise, not theirs. Once children are exposed to that forbidden fruit, worldly experience, they no longer function as the window onto innocence and simplicity we desire them to be. The paradise they reconstruct for us is bought with deception. Knowledge, in this case, is power, and adults, with their sole claim upon knowledge, share with God the proverbial sovereign power to banish and send into exile the despoiled innocents we create.

This chapter picks up the nexus between power and knowledge as theorised by the philosopher and historian Michel Foucault. A protégé of Louis Althusser (see chapter 3), Foucault is one of the most influential French intellectuals to have emerged from the politically charged scene of May 1968. Foucault reverses the knowledge is power idiom to produce instead the more ambiguous phrase, 'Power is knowledge'. Foucault's claim is not that to possess knowledge is to have power over others, although this may also be true. Rather, he develops a notion of power not only as repressive or coercive, but also as producing knowledge and social practices. Power, for Foucault, organises life through knowledges (discourses) such as psychology, medicine and demography, and institutions such as the law, school and family.

Our interest here is not so much how adults control children by withholding information. Rather, this chapter explores how disciplines, sciences and the social practices on which they depend create the ideal of the innocent, normal, child. If we view innocent childhood as historically and socially constructed rather than as a natural given – as an idea that developed in tandem with a host of knowledges about human essence and behaviour – then we can discern why that idea has taken such a hold of our imaginations. Why, in other words, childhood innocence has become so indispensable to our culture: as its prehistory and goal, its meaning, anxiety and eternal panacea.

## The history of sexuality and other discourses of childhood

Once mere chattels of the household head and a valuable source of labour, children are now regarded as priceless, innocent bearers of humanity's future, not to be burdened by work or any other adult concern. How and why has this change taken place? We find that the vicissitudes of childhood are tied to broader cultural trends and a fundamental change to the way individuals imagine themselves. Having transformed our thinking about the relationship between identity and cultural change, Foucault is helpful here.

According to Foucault, from around the 18th century a social and political shift gradually took shape. Power came predominantly to express itself not as a power to let live and make die (through the sovereign's prerogative to kill his subjects), but rather as a power to *'foster* life or *disallow* it to the point of death'.[1] This means that power ceases primarily to be exercised punitively, and instead comes to foster different ways of being – to facilitate life. The penal system, for example, begins to show an interest in the criminal's conscience, investing more resources into rehabilitation and discipline than punishment. The death penalty makes less sense now not because we are more compassionate, but because power is currently exercised through the management of life rather than its cessation.[2]

No longer located above social relations in the figure of the king, power in liberal democracies disperses and proliferates through social institutions (parliaments, universities, government departments, NGOs and multinational corporations), interpersonal relationships and our very bodies. By means of these various relationships, power orders and coordinates life rather than suppresses it. At the levels of the individual and of the population, power is what within us speaks the truth of our identity and desire, and this truth, in turn, provides data for the discovery of demographic trends. In this age of biopower we are no longer 'the masses', an amorphous, poor body vulnerable to the monarch's whim. We are individuals, ready to declare who we are and what we want to any government, university or market researcher who takes an interest. Power in contemporary life is exercised at the point of enjoyment, freedom and the declaration of one's individuality. Power is knowledge because, through knowledge of the self, power increases its field of influence, provoking new forms of self-consciousness, desire and identity. While the medieval king could only deprive his subjects of life, today the most minute details of citizens' lives are mapped and organised; we willingly yield ourselves as data in the name of the good of society: public health, consumer freedom, and law and order.

Knowledge is the apparatus through which such ordering is achieved. The academic disciplines, which also begin to proliferate during the 18th century, divide the world and humanity into neatly discrete dichotomies. In the last 300 years not only has the body become an object of study, but so also has the soul, along with every aspect of behaviour in between. A particularly fruitful object of the production of knowledge, and thereby of power, has been sexuality. Foucault famously argues against widespread opinion that in the Victorian era sexuality was repressed, whereas it had once flowed freely. In fact, he counters, this period produced the many varieties of sexuality that today we understand as lying at the core of personal identity. The silence that apparently shrouded sexuality in the 19th and early 20th centuries was, instead, an important stratagem through which biopower incites discourse – speech, writing, knowledges – about sexuality. Victorians may have been

> deprived of a certain way of speaking about sex, a mode that was disallowed as being too direct, crude, or coarse. But this was only the counterpart of other discourses, and perhaps the condition necessary in order for them to function . . .[3]

The silence we put down to repression interacts with other more refined and technical discourses about sex, and even intensifies interest in it (as with furtive, sexually charged whispers between inmates of a boarding school, the prohibition of their speech is what renders it delightful). Through this interaction between silence and technical speech, we came to define the so-called perversions (including homosexuality, 'the love that dare not speak its name'). We came also to decide what characterises normal sexual feeling and behaviour, and the stages of sexual maturation. In the wake of these exhaustive investigations into human sexual behaviour, sexuality is now viewed as the most natural, yet scientific, aspect of human being. (The incitement to discourse of the apparent embargo on sexual expression now saturates Western culture in the form of reality television and progenitors such as Oprah, where the truth of an individual is revealed and their sins redeemed through confessions of their sexual peccadilloes.)

Foucault shows us, then, that sex was never repressed so much as redeployed to a new task: the investment of biopower in contemporary citizens, who then make themselves available to medicine, psychology, the law and popular culture by declaring who they are according to a metrics of bodily desire. By overcoming an imagined repression, the subject feels that they are speaking back to power, whereas actually they are contributing to the bank of knowledge through which power regulates experience.

But what has this to do with children, who are, after all, so very removed from sexuality? Significantly, the strategic silence that prompted a more technical and searching investigation of sex settled most heavily upon children. At this time, when sexuality was carved up and named, children were also reconceived as sexuality-free zones, which occurred through a variety of apparently contradictory discourses and silences. The sanitisation of the child was achieved in practice where, for instance, children were vigilantly supervised – sleeping and bathing arrangements carefully administered – to prevent the possibility of masturbation (considered a hazard to the individual and to society). It was symbolically achieved through a literature in which the myth of childhood innocence was further refined (after the fashion of Rousseau's *Émile*) to become evermore ethereal in the figure of, for instance, Brontë's Helen Burns (Jane Eyre's angelic but sickly friend) or J. M. Barrie's more carefree, but equally otherworldly, Peter Pan. These eternal children are kept innocent of sexuality because they can never grow up.[4] While Burns fades into a premature death, Pan is sentenced to eternal childhood in his timeless prison, Neverland. It is through these figures that we are allowed to believe in an everlasting childhood innocence that compensates adults their growing old.

Ironically, a conspicuous effect of purging the child of sexuality was that their sexual significance was intensified. Like the silent repression that acted as a motive force for the proliferation of sexualities, this re-imagining of childhood gave it a heightened quality in relation to sexuality. The place of childhood innocence materialising alongside the sexualities set it apart from sexuality, while also constantly referring to it. The ideal of childhood innocence is permeated by a sexual resonance because, not in spite, of its purification of sexuality, a purification that is continually re-enacted through our knowledges and practices regarding children. Children are not simply non-sexual; rather, they are constructed as such through constant surveillance by adults for signs of premature sexuality. Their lives are managed in order to forestall the possibility of sexuality, and so children become the apparently asexual bearers of sexual meaning.

Through the very specific knowledges and practices yielded by the post-Enlightenment concern for ordering life – the biological sciences, psychology, education, justice, humanitarian interventions – the child is now drenched in sexuality. Always at risk of sexual exploitation, the ideal of innocence could not but eventually take on a sexual cast. Today the innocent child is that constitutive silence that for Foucault organises the discourse of sexuality, a silence that, given current anxieties about the precocity and abuse of children, is increasingly voluble about sex.

Children's social significance is, then, at least in part due to the role of childhood in shoring up adult fantasy and identity. The institution that invests children with this role is, predominantly, the family.

## 'Everyone just . . . pretend to be normal': the normative power of the family

This advice from the film *Little Miss Sunshine* is issued by Richard Hoover, the diligent, if hapless, patriarch of a typically dysfunctional family unit. Hoover's plea to his family – to 'pretend to be normal' – brings to light the gap between his actual life and the rigid advice he preaches as a motivational speaker. ('There are two kinds of people in this world, winners and losers', he continually lectures. The only question being on which side of this divide does Richard Hoover fall?) Yet the phrase – 'Everyone just pretend to be normal' – also rings true for viewers, and has received a second life as a popular slogan adorning T-shirts, coffee mugs and baseball caps. There is clearly a more general sense of non-compliance to a norm felt by people identifying with this catchphrase. The absurdity of there being a normal way of being that most people feel eludes them is epitomised by the Hoovers' failure as a regulative institution, that is, as a family.

This anxiety about not being normal puts a great deal of pressure on children in particular, who carry the burden of their parents' hopes for a harmonious, emotionally fulfilling family life. We are frequently subjected to aspirational images of well turned out children and tidy homes, suspended delectably before us in magazines and television advertising. We want to be those people, but also sense the impossibility of such idyllic familial bliss, of infinitely energetic, available, reasonable parents and relentlessly cute and respectful children. This tension between the ideal and the experience of family life accounts for the success of the dysfunctional family motif in popular culture, not only in the Hoover family, but also in the Simpsons, the Bundys (*Married With Children*), the Wilkersons (*Malcolm in the Middle*), the Gallaghers (*Shameless*), the Pritchetts (*Modern Family*) and the Australian Heslops (*Muriel's Wedding*). Our enjoyment of their dysfunction (and the shameful antics that issue from it) relies on a partial identification with their botched attempts at domestic unity. We watch in horror and with relief as each character inevitably plays out deviance from their allotted role within the family, despite a grim determination to make things work. They illustrate the struggle we all feel when attempting to be an individual within a social frame that demands conformity and compromise.

This tension between individuality and conformity is, indeed, a defining feature of the contemporary family, and the child, as both a site of burgeoning personal experience and of civilisation, represents the meeting point of these conflicting demands. The bourgeois family's paradoxical charter is to nurture individual difference while also preparing the individual for social compliance. Liberal tradition sees the family hearth as a safe haven to freely pursue enjoyment and develop natural capacities (see chapter 3). Through the emergence of a middle class during the Industrial Revolution, the family came to be defined through blood and affection rather than relations of production.[5] Thus the family is imagined to be outside commercial society and the state, or as a state of nature within the state, whose interests compete with those of government. But the family is also the setting in which we are first charged with a social role and binding responsibilities to others.

In the family, then, we find a curious double apparatus: the family individualises its members by withdrawing them from other power mechanisms (the factory, the office, the school, the hospital, and so forth) and giving them a sense of meaning and purpose beyond an impersonal social function. But the family also supports and reinforces these mechanisms by applying the same levelling classifications within the home as medicine or education does outside it. This is the family's normative function, its task in bringing its members into line (in Latin 'norm' means to square, or standardise). Far from being a refuge from the scrutiny of social institutions, the family is an optimal instrument of social surveillance. Such surveillance takes place through the penetration of professional discourses into the home. That the family medical encyclopaedia and popularised child developmental manual have infiltrated the home library demonstrates this. The parent is a trained amateur scientist, expected to consult the latest know-how and to recognise where their child fits on the bell curve of weight, height, behaviour and intelligence.[6]

So the concerns of the state are not excluded from the family home, but are concentrated within it. Perhaps the most publicly noted new presence of government in the Australian family of recent years has been the Baby Bonus, a crude, yet relatively popular pronatalist (population-boosting) policy instrument. Although first introduced by the 1912 Fisher government, the political figure usually associated with this windfall is former Treasurer Peter Costello. Public response to inclusion of the bonus in the 2004 Budget was mixed. Some people resented what they felt was the treasurer's presence in their boudoir, while others were wary of a more general family focus of government policy. Yet many enthusiastically took up the charge of procreating, which accounted for $780 million of the national budget in 2005 alone.[7] International evidence suggests, however, that bonuses affect the timing rather than number of births,[8] and Australian women already game the system by engaging in risky attempts to delay birth to the next financial year because if they do so they will receive larger payments.[9] Policy that attempts to alter the course of citizens' lives can sometimes have perverse effects on reproductive behaviour.

That said, the influence of state concerns (such as population and health) on family life is generally far subtler than this instance suggests, enacted at the apparently independent level of personal preference and in relation to less tangible rewards than a one-off cash payment. There is a particularly mawkish scene in Disney's *101 Dalmatians* that exemplifies the force of social imperatives upon individual experience. Anita and her nanny sit at the kitchen table. The nanny explains how she knows the dog, Perdita, is going to have puppies. She explains the significance of the gleam in Perdita's eye, and the gentleness of her expression, as the camera pans to Anita's face – which also reflects these telltale signs – and the viewer realises that she, too, is pregnant. What the film shows through this fetishisation of pregnancy is the promised fulfilment the prospective child symbolises. Anita looks content; the film portrays her maternity as the missing piece that will complete her. Anita, Roger, their dogs and, indeed, the unexplained presence of a nanny, comprise a family waiting to happen (just add the child). Although pregnancy is presented here less as a choice than a spot of good luck, this scene attempts to summarise the intimacy of the decision to have children. Within this decision is the hope that a child will increase the social value of the soon to be parents and fulfil a personal trajectory that would otherwise remain unexplored. The decision is experienced as a personal development, and apparently only incidentally fulfils the political function of increasing population. Yet this is how we internalise social imperatives and make them our own. Even without the disconcerting spectre of Peter Costello at the bedroom window, his work is already done by a social imaginary that holds children to be invaluable. The Baby Bonus was an unnecessary inducement; population growth was already assured by the sense of personal worth gained from being in the family way.[10]

Once children are born, these internalised social functions kick in most forcefully through the playing of roles and following of scripts that penetrate our personalities and change who we are. (This is when the realisation that you're a parent resembles *Invasion of the Body Snatchers* rather than *101 Dalmatians*.) These automatically assumed roles seem natural, hence the belief in maternal instinct. But for most first-time mothers, motherhood is a position they occupy anxiously and experience via the criticism and approval of their mothers, mothers-in-law, friends, siblings, maternal health nurses, neighbours and perfect strangers. Everyone has an interest in how mummy and baby are doing, and as time passes and the maternal role comes to be normalised, the community's interest is gradually withdrawn.

Once we convincingly inhabit our parental roles, enacting them in accordance with community standards, we are ready to be a family. For we not only inhabit these formal functions, but they also inhabit us through the gentle persuasion of others' attention and surveillance, which we then internalise. Being a good parent means having the legitimacy to inculcate one's children with civilising values through love, caring attention and surveillance. It is the very personal nature of this investment in children, not only of time and money, but also of emotions, freedoms, hopes, dreams and sense of self, that is indispensable to the social order. Without these intangible dividends of parenthood there would be no investment in children. But however much we love our children, the work of parenthood is to turn out citizens, individuals only to the extent that their personal desires and preferences can be addressed by socially approved outlets (shopping, voting, four weeks annual recreation leave, Friday night happy hour and heterosexual coupling). Citizens are allowed – even encouraged – to be individuals, but in prescribed ways and in their own time.

The technically dysfunctional family is the family that fails to turn out citizens, and so neglects to be normative. The effects on children of such breakdown (from the overly responsible caretaker child, to disruptive, invisible or manipulative children) are widely studied by the kinds of discursive power that will be discussed at greater length in the next section; family dysfunction is a core concern of state welfare (institutional power). Tragedies emerging from dysfunctional family set-ups receive a great deal of media and political censure. There is no circumstance in which it is considered alright to neglect and inflict suffering on children. That being the case, it is curious, then, that family dysfunction is such a mainstay of situation comedy and reality television. What does this fascination indicate? And why do we so enjoy watching the hopeless inadequacy of others' family lives?

The television dysfunctional family helps us manage the conflicting emotions and identifications experienced in our family relationships and the anxiety caused by others' judgements upon us. These programs sometimes tell a cautionary tale about parental decisions that seem logical only from the viewpoint of short-term gain (parents, we are told, should think long term). In an episode of *The*

*Simpsons*, for instance, Homer caves into Bart and Lisa's demands after three days solid of nagging. We chuckle smugly when Homer asks: 'Will you stop nagging me if I say I'll take you to Krustyland?', knowing that in doing so he is creating a rod for his own back. This is a strange instance of identification: viewers sympathise with the dysfunctional father and feel superior to him. There are occasions for a more uncomfortable enjoyment when we negotiate through the sitcom the inevitable moment of being judged by others to be bad parents. Virtually any scene from *The Simpsons* or *Malcolm in the Middle* where the family is in public summarises the pain and embarrassment of being watched and appraised by other parents. The sitcom allows us to laugh at ourselves through the travails of others.

Conversely, reality television is a pure indulgence of our need to feel superior to others' parental ineptitude. Shows such as *Super Nanny* have a decidedly punitive tone, pandering to the more sadistic normative sentiments. In viewing these programs viewers enjoy the privilege of condemning the behaviour of both children and parents, and feel the pleasure of not being judged themselves. The recent balloon boy hoax in the United States is particularly interesting in the light of this aspect of reality television. The incident began when the Heene family reported their six year old son, Falcon, missing; he was believed to have floated away in a large homemade helium balloon. The media and the American public anxiously followed the balloon across Colorado, and several airplanes were diverted and cancelled before it landed . . . empty. When Falcon emerged from a secret hiding place at home, the family expressed its relief and joy. By the following day the Heenes' story was unravelling: Falcon unwittingly admitted in a live interview that it was a hoax staged to create publicity for their own reality show.[11] In their determination to be ordained exemplars of good parenting, the Heenes rapidly became America's worst parents. It was even suggested that their three children should be taken into care.

The Heenes' take-home lesson was that it is almost impossible to be a real family in the media and appear in a good light (particularly if you ask your children to collaborate in a media hoax). The era of the Bradys,[12] *The Partridge Family* and the Huxtables (*The Cosby Show*) is well and truly over. Since then, Marcia Brady's been to rehab, Danny Partridge has been homeless, Denise Huxtable's done soft porn and we no longer find parables of domestic perfection convincing. The family as it is predominantly represented in the media today is flawed, and to the extent that we see ideal families, this is usually as parody (for example, *The Brady Bunch Movie*), or emphasises the disquiet at the heart of that family ideal (the Drapers of *Mad Men*). The new amiable family that solicits our identification is dysfunctional – not too dysfunctional, mind, but only to the extent that its experience resonates with the pressures of contemporary domestic life. Sitcom dysfunction is more plausible than sitcom perfection; it also continues to fulfil a normative task by regulating us in a more complicated manner.

For beyond all this getting real the sit com pretends, the role of comedy is still to uplift and resolve the tensions that otherwise would lead family dysfunction to tragedy. The comedy, whether in television or film, ultimately climaxes with an expression of redemptive family love. This is a familiar resolution for *The Simpsons* that continually brings them back from the brink of collapse and makes us feel good about identification with them. For who, in the final analysis, has more sex than Marge and Homer? What siblings care for each other more than Lisa and Bart? *Little Miss Sunshine*, again, shows the progress of a family from the verge of failure, to redemption through love for one another, and the catalyst for this expression of harmony is seven year old Olive. What the Hoovers are able to represent through their dysfunction is the double bind of family life: the family supports political life by containing the struggle through which individuals put aside their particular desires to become members of broader society. This is why the family is seen as the social glue of a community (and anxieties about the future of a social group focus on relationships within the family. Do children obey their parents? Are women in the home enough? Are families staying together?).

But the family also becomes a site of resistance against society because of what they need to do to support it: the family hearth is also an abject sphere, mopping up the economic, psychological and emotional expenditure through which the citizen is created. The family enables a separation within the self whereby bodily life (anger, love, melancholy, sex, sleep, nourishment) does not lag behind the citizen once they enter the public sphere. The family keeps back from public view an unwanted remainder of the self, which is why families are so frequently a source of embarrassment, even of horror. There is an anxiety that a usually hidden aspect of oneself will show when family is around: the emotional struggles through which individuals emerge might become obvious to colleagues or friends, for instance. The horror of the mother who displays snaps of her daughter's naked babyhood to all comers is an acute, if hackneyed, representation of this fear.

The most celebrated moment of *Little Miss Sunshine* shows Olive finally dancing for the child beauty pageant she and her family travelled across America to attend. Through her performance a family secret is revealed: Grandpa, who showed her these moves, was a studious observer of strip club burlesque, and Olive innocently reproduces this genre before an increasingly incensed audience of regular pageant goers. Besides this family secret, the beauty pageant community is shown a secret of their own: that pageantry sexualises their daughters. Some fairly crude signifiers of innocence barely obscure the sexual connotations of these performances (see chapter 2), which many (more middle-class) viewers find abject. Olive confronts them with this aspect of the pageant, thereby provoking their ire: they find her performance unwatchable.

Amid boos and jeers, an astonishing event of family bonding takes place: one by one, the Hoovers join Olive's dance, in collective resistance against the pageant community. It is clear from the narrative that seven year old Olive resists no social paradigm; she simply loves dancing and innocently imagines herself a beauty queen. But through her innocence, the family finally finds their belonging together. It is a belonging that thwarts and triumphs over the normative ideals of American beauty and of familial perfection. And that's why fans love the Hoovers (as YouTube emulations of Olive's dance testify).

Notably, though, Olive, as the innocent child who unknowingly behaves as its catalyst, is subtly excluded from the Hoovers' act of rebellion. It is somehow unimaginable that a child such as Olive might deliberately question the norms through which she is judged. Olive's purity prepares the way for her family's redemption. But do they take her with them into their embrace of imperfection? Or is she simply carried through the ordeal? Does Olive remain oblivious, and in the thrall of the beauty pageant ideal? The child is here situated as an agent of others' change, but not her own. This quality is what we have come to expect from children, through whom adults seek their own dysfunction, to solve their own problems. The child is, however, also subject to social pressures, our conception of them a product of cultural necessities. Let's, then, test the certainty of our knowledge of childhood.

## The child under the microscope

In seeking to understand why the child is lately such a focus of concern, we can learn much from the growth of knowledges about childhood. It is fair to say that parents learnt to worry about children from experts who, striving to develop explanations and solve the problems of society in general, turned to the study of children. Theories developed in the rarefied sphere of the laboratory are now taken for granted as practically applicable within the school, the childcare centre and the family home. Emphasis is usually placed upon our potential for failure as parents, teachers or childcare workers, and the damage wrought by improper care of the child (too clingy or too distant, overindulgent or negligent, too permissive or too strict). The child's world had become such a delicate ecosystem that it is almost inevitable that our children will find their way either to a psychiatrist or to prison. The child is seen through a lens trained on solving social problems, and thereby becomes a social problem.

It's also worth remembering that the studies that yielded these truths about children were oriented towards solving a broader social problem, the issue of governing individuals as populations. Within the frame of social research, children were positioned as this problem and its ambiguous solution. 'The child' as we now know it is a product of these discourses, reduced to a manageable quantity, fed through an abstract framework that makes sense of otherwise diffuse and meaningless behaviours and finally turned out as good or bad, functional or dysfunctional, normal or slow. Given the problem-oriented social milieu within which such knowledge is produced, is it any wonder that we worry about children?

Knowledges about children emerged alongside the social institutions that administer them and each proclaims as its particular remit the welfare of the child. At the pointy end of child-protection and child-purification movements were schools and workhouses, law courts, the child-labour reform movement and child savers more generally, all attempting to rescue children of the poor from harm, certainly, but most powerfully, rhetorically, from 'premature worldliness'.[13] By sorting children, these institutions attempted to prepare the ground for a well-ordered society, a society that knows about its citizenry and within which each knows their proper place. Yet to sort a population, these institutions needed to have developed conceptual machinery for knowing it, areas of expertise that mapped the range of individuals' possible interactions by the coordinates of family, class, community and nation. The emerging fields of psychology and psychoanalysis, medical hygienism, social work and economics developed insights about patient populations by focusing upon a relatively captive sample: children.

Children had become more available to these investigators through the founding of institutions that collected them in one place and under one gaze: the school, the orphanage and the reformatory. Nowadays we take for granted that schoolchildren will be observed; we find unremarkable the presence of researchers with clipboards, finely calibrating inclass behaviour. Back when childcare and education were cruder sciences, it was observed that while some children flourished with little attention, others resisted pedagogy and discipline. And these 'problem' children were thought to exemplify a problem population, or underclass, whose value to society was uncertain. These children became sites of anxiety, righteous sermon and rigorous study. Moral panics in 1950s Australia regarding bodgies and widgies are a case in point, as newspapers decried the gender confusion, promiscuity and delinquency of working-class youths and academics developed theories about their portent for greater society.[14]

The science of childhood emerged less from a sense of care for children than a need to produce social norms and to contain social anomaly. The progress of normative ideas about the assessment of children (according to age and stage of development) responded to a broader program of social management. There was a desire to control the life of the population, to nurture some parts of the social organism while isolating others through segregation, detention and even sterilisation.[15] Children considered backward or feeble minded had to be kept in check, their degeneracy controlled for fear they may contaminate others.

Once channelled through remedial institutions, a role could be found for them that would diminish the harm to the community they apparently epitomised.[16] (In the contemporary context, the best possible outcome for problem children is to be diagnosed, medicated, segregated and finally mainstreamed. At worst, they become a legal, rather than educational, problem, entering another system of institutional regulation.)

Yet children are not only regarded as sources of potential trouble to be neutralised; chapter 5 will turn again to these 'fallen children'. Children of the middle classes (demonstrating neither the effects of social disadvantage nor overindulgence) were, from the beginning, also subjects of scientific interest, but as imperilled objects in need of protection from a volatile environment. Conceived of as already neutral, these children were blank slates upon which the community could write its hopes for the future. Cushioned from the kinds of experience that would ruin them, these children represented for the human sciences a controlled field of experimentation, alienated from the rest of society the better to yield data about human potential. Where freedom was increasingly defined in terms of the desires of the individual, the locus of power also became the individual. The middle-class child was considered the individual *par excellence*, unsullied by a political and social context. This is also why the child is the focus of knowledge about humanity. A simpler, more ideal version of man, the child came to represent the innocence of a human life unlived, a pure potentiality of the person in laboratory conditions. By focusing upon individuals supposedly uncontaminated by the effects of society, it was assumed more reliable truths about humankind could be gleaned through the study and cultivation of children (the child graduates from the nursery to school and the Scouts, an apparently neutral culture medium for the fruition of adults' dreams of success and empire).

We fail to grasp anxiety about children, then, outside this more pervasive interest in the question of our essence as humans. Once the search was on for the fundamental nature of the human individual, scientific interest concentrated on the child, imagining it to be the simplest unit of humankind and analysis. The view that children represented the origins and essence of adulthood was summarised in the 19th century by the catchy slogan 'Ontogeny recapitulates phylogeny', borrowed from the biological sciences and applied to other areas of life. The biogenetic law, as it is known, was the neat idea that the stages of an individual's development mirror the evolution of the species. In biology, this notion was often demonstrated by the stages of foetal development because at one point or another the embryo resembles all the animal stages we might have passed through before reaching the human form (fish, salamander, tortoise, hog, chick, etc.).

When applied to culture, recapitulation is used to support the even more tenuous idea of social evolution. According to this view, if the individual repeats the path taken by Western culture, children would be equivalent to so-called primitive peoples and become more civilised as they mature. Apart from its obvious offence against tribal peoples, this notion presents children as key to social science. As we saw in chapter 3, to understand the fundaments of social man, Enlightenment thinkers looked to the savage and the child. Likewise, in the 19th and 20th centuries, the search for the optimal (that is, most productive) arrangement of individuals into society led to the primitive child.

As with contemporary discourse about the stem cell, the child's specific character was understood as yet to be determined, making them ideal subjects for experimentation and for fantasy. The laboratory for such experimentation is the school or nursery (parents, too, are trained to scrutinise and categorise their child's every movement and desire through the discourse of the parenting manual). The child's social relationships are thus controlled, adjusted and monitored, data sets are generated, theories formulated and a general theory of the individual in society is inferred from this evidence.

One of the most influential discourses to take the middle class child as its unit of analysis is Freudian psychoanalysis. Significantly, the psychoanalytic story is also notoriously sex obsessed, producing the child alongside an evermore pathologised sexuality. Freud argued that qualities associated with culture – language, conscience, compassion, art, music and literature – are but refined diversions 'sublimations' of sexual energy. From infancy, Freud argued, we learn to manage the libido, which to begin with is uncontrollable, painful and insatiable. Psychoanalysis tested the notion of idealised childhood innocence, even while further escalating its cultural cachet. Since psychoanalysis, the child has become the centre of individual experience and the focus of personal existential examination.

This crucial moment for the importance of childhood innocence deepened ambivalence about children. Freud directly challenged comfortable notions about childhood innocence, particularly the view that sexuality is absent from childhood, emerging only at the onset of puberty. But Freud argued that even those first stirrings of feeling through which the infant establishes a connection to the world (and especially to its mother) have a sexual character. Such scandalous association between infancy and sexuality was the theoretical counterpart to a sexualising surveillance of children, threads that Foucault draws together in his *History of Sexuality*.[17]

Significantly, though, Freudian theory also disarmed sexuality of its salacious meaning. Generalised to apply to all dimensions of life, sex lost its power as a marker of transgression. If Freud stripped the child of its innocence, then he also rendered sexuality more banal. Sex and adulthood came to appear more infantile, even innocent. What Freud called 'the talking cure' reacquainted adults with a lost childhood vulnerability and allowed them to identify with a childhood self.

In this way Freud's talking cure is, in Foucault's terms, an 'incitement to discourse' that weaves a narrative and connects previously disparate ideas and practices so that new styles of being and of desiring become possible. In particular, the clinical emphasis upon adults' childlike vulnerability and lack of mastery bears an interesting relation to the child's course in contemporary knowledge discourses. 'The child' now symbolises a dependency that belongs to all of us, but which liberal ideals of self-sufficiency and personal responsibility repudiate. Adults prefer to experience vulnerability at one remove, through ideals of childhood. Psychoanalysis traces back adults' fragility to a series of events occurring during childhood. Psychoanalysis represents the perfect storm of this fraught relation between representations of adulthood and childhood because it so precariously balances the sexualised child and infantilised adult, because while psychoanalysis profanes children by associating them with sexuality, it also restores the patient (or analysand) to the innocence of childhood. The childhood self of Freud's clinic is the wounded centre of human experience.

For the analyst, the adult is an extension of the child, and the child bears within it the seeds of adult dysfunction. The human sciences' privileging of the child as an object of study signals an interest in ourselves. Freud summarises well this search for human origins that discovers its most intimate truth in the child when he writes that

> writers who concern themselves with explaining the characteristics and reactions of the adult have devoted much more attention to the primeval period which is comprised in the life of the individual's ancestors . . . than to the other primeval period, which falls within the lifetime of the individual himself – that is, to childhood.[18]

Here Freud imagines the child as the kernel of the adult, in similar rhetorical fashion to the earlier biogenetic law.[19] For Freud and those he has influenced, the most subtle familial dynamics are impressed upon the child, writ large upon the adult psyche, and then played out in the adult's ability (or inability) to cope with life. The child effectively stands for the fragility felt by adults in their everyday dealings with others in their social sphere. Mention of the inner child in self-help books and on daytime television is a popular expression of this principle: it refers to that part of the self that feels liable to injury or carries a wound that leads to dysfunction. Likewise, in the hands of psychological experimenters, the child becomes prone to separation anxiety,[20] schism and distress,[21] hot housing[22] and 'helicopter parenting',[23] each of which is said to damage children in unique ways. Childhood thus becomes synonymous with injury and embodies the fears of abandonment we all feel, but which are deflected upon children.

If we worry about children and feel somewhat emotionally divided about them it is because the child is both the object and a product of the knowledges and institutions that support our way of life, liberal democracy. The child is a blank slate upon which individualist fantasies of freedom are projected, and in order to play this role it must appear natural, clean and innocent. Yet, paradoxically, by virtue of its innocence, the child embodies both individual autonomy and the vulnerability all feel but often do not admit. Ideas regarding children are symptoms of a deep inconsistency at the heart of contemporary society and the liberal ideals that guide who we think we are. As literary theorist Caroline Levander observes, we can 'chart liberalism's inner workings' through representations of childhood because the child simultaneously represents liberalism's 'promise of autonomy and the reality of [our mutual] dependence'.[24] This means the child becomes the focus not only of the most idealistic notions of who we are and what we stand for (courage, compassion, independence, freedom, democracy), but also our most intimate fears of frailty, loneliness and social collapse. By focusing on a characterisation of children as weak and dependent, adults stabilise their self-conception as in control, as problem solvers and protectors.

Adults' repudiation of vulnerability in relation to the fallen child, will now be explored in chapter 5.

# Chapter 5
## Fallen innocents
### Adolescents, Aboriginal and stateless children

In the preceding chapters we explored the relationship between notions of childhood innocence and the construction of adult identity and desire in the commercial and political spheres and in the realm of fantasy. This chapter considers the consequences of such idealisation borne by those who do not quite fit this ideal, such as teenagers, Indigenous children and refugee children. Their raw vulnerability threatens the sanctity of childhood, and in so doing, undermines the meaning of adulthood and community in Australia.

These groups fall foul of innocence for different reasons. Adolescence is a time of transition from childhood innocence to adult knowledge. Teenagers make us feel uneasy because they are exposed (and expose themselves) to risks they are still learning to negotiate. They disrupt the comfortable equilibrium associated with younger children. No longer fitting that identity, they test its boundaries and break away from parental authority. In the face of the challenges this independence incurs, teenagers render their parents helpless, and this sense of helplessness and instability feels like a kind of evil.

Indeed, the adolescent's progress is like the fall from paradise (occasioned by disobedience) from which evil is said to originate. Like God the creator, we birth, love and protect our children, and in so doing make them the lovable, compliant, innocent products of our creation fantasies. Once our protective edifices can no longer limit their curiosity, children become disobedient, disorderly, hormonal and a danger to themselves and the community. It is because the ideal of innocence can no longer contain them that teenagers come to threaten it.

The reasons Indigenous and refugee children threaten childhood – and Australian – innocence is somewhat different. There are still issues of control at stake, the control of a cultural minority through a stated concern for the protection of their children. Such attempts are rhetorically unstable. The material conditions of these children cannot support the rarefied fantasy of childhood innocence. The language of protection verges into a demonisation of children, viewed as already a lost cause and as bad seeds. Such children do not fall from a state of innocence, as the does adolescent; rather, they are pushed.

Australian communities and governments feel guilty, frustrated and threatened by children in situations of poverty and danger, not only because we don't like children to be at risk, but also because their existence gives the lie to a myth that sustains and justifies how we exist as adults. Just as Western affluence is possible only by virtue of the historical dispossession of non-Western peoples, the innocence of Western, privileged childhood is bought with the innocence of underprivileged children. Third-world children uncannily reveal a way of life and an illusion of control that cannot be maintained without sacrifice: they are the sacrifice.

Disadvantaged children cause discomfort because they do not share the privileges that are supposed to be children's right. They are also the most visible face of a more general need shared by their families and communities. Australians' somewhat peculiar response to endemic poverty is frequently to cast an apolitical and deeply moralising net over it, to blame the parents in order to save the child. For decades Aboriginal children were removed from their families, and then subjected to an institutionalised upbringing that often left them traumatised and alienated from community and culture. Despite these patently damaging effects, the language used to justify the policy of removal appealed to the welfare of these children. A deeply paternalistic assumption that removing Indigenous children gave them a better life continued to operate in the face of evidence to the contrary. Meanwhile, their parents' grief and trauma was belittled with the mantra that (like animals) they would soon forget.

There has been a tendency to pit refugee children's interests against those of their parents too, to frame the child as victim of parents' selfish greed rather than as belonging to the very community we vilify. That 'boat people' would throw their children overboard to emotionally blackmail the Australian navy is only conceivable if the desperate situations from which they run are overlooked. Refugees love their children too, and the attempt to obscure this fact signals a greater evasion of responsibility for the children and their parents once they reach our shores.

Each case shows that political rhetoric and policy can be animated by the fantasy of childhood innocence, with far-reaching effects for those involved. Where children put into question a sanitised, sentimental notion of innocence, interventions are launched to save them, irrespective of their communities' interests. Such rescue missions affect a purification of the social field, where the child who fails to measure up to ideals of innocence is cleaned away like so much debris. Let us first examine this psychological response to socially marginalised children before embarking upon a closer consideration of adolescence, the Stolen Generations and immigrant children.

## Children out of place: identity and contamination

Invoking the idea of innocence is not only a means of treasuring children, but is also an instrument of social control. As we have seen already, the value of childhood innocence structures notions of citizenship and gives the community a sense of purpose. The Australian way of life strives towards an ideal of perfected enjoyment protected from politics, violence, poverty and sexuality, and children are the placeholders of this hallowed realm. Because the idea of childhood innocence gives significance to Western life, images of children affect how we evaluate our society. That children are exposed to harm on our watch troubles community morale, as it should. But Western communities often respond hastily in the face of juvenile vulnerability, choosing actions that allay adult anxiety over actions that would attend to these children's needs. This response frequently involves removing them from public view into state care or offshore detention, an out of sight, out of mind approach that does more to preserve the idea of childhood innocence than the wellbeing of actual children. Social anthropologist Mary Douglas can help us understand how this is allowed to occur.

Douglas argues that cultural systems of meaning and value are organised by notions of purity and danger; what causes most moral upset, fear and anxiety is the threat of pollution or disorder. Through what Douglas calls the 'creative movement' of ordering our environment, we provide ourselves with a 'unity of experience' in the face of things ultimately beyond our control.[1] By compartmentalising our surroundings, we manage our identity in relation to others who influence us and downplay the social nature of personal identity. A hair in one's soup, dirty dishes on the bedroom floor or piles of old newspapers cluttering the livingroom cause anxiety because they represent disorder and ambiguity, experienced as a threat to one's own integrity of self. Things and behaviours are dirty not by dint of some essential property, but because they offend a sense of order. Dirt, according to Douglas, is 'matter out of place',[2] so that things found where, according to convention, they shouldn't be provoke discomfort or even disgust. The only way to set the world right again – and to preserve a sense of one's proper place – is to remove the deviant object (thereby restoring purity).

Douglas supplies a poignant anthropological example from the Nuer, a tribe of western Ethiopia and southern Sudan. When confronted with a monstrous birth – the birth of a child who falls outside what is considered healthy or normal – the Nuer were anxious to restore the cosmological order set off balance by this event. To this end, they classified such children as 'baby hippopotamuses, accidentally born to humans and, with this labelling, the appropriate action is clear. They gently lay them in the river where they belong'.[3] Fear of the unknown is patched over by this hasty recategorisation: the baby whose difference is so unsettling is neutralised by this reinterpretation of their birth. It was an accident; the baby really belongs to another species. The child whom the Nuer cannot recognise as their own – who provokes unease about their identity and what it is to be human – is thus tenderly, horribly, sacrificed for the good of the whole.

This action seems irresponsible, even barbaric. Yet, is our society so very different?

Children, conceived of as innocent, are our most precious and purified of social resources. By treasuring our children and protecting them from ambiguous (threatening) social relations, we signal to ourselves that our way of life is better than others' where childhood is put at risk. Innocent childhood is produced and preserved through this separation from conflict, work and desire, all of which complicate and disorganise adult life. Thus we exalt childhood and give our children the better (purer) life we cannot live ourselves.

But for this reason, a child found out of this rarefied context provokes repugnance and fear, and must be removed from the sphere of concern to restore the social order. This separation is necessary to maintain the ideal of childhood innocence that sanctifies the Western way of life. Our identity as a community depends upon it. The following examples should clarify how this ritualised cleansing comes to pass.

## Adolescents: public enemies or babes in the woods?

Adolescents clutter public space with their idle, unsupervised presence. They hang out at the mall and don't spend, at the playground and don't play. Wherever shall we put them?

The British public is currently at war with its own youth. In 2006 their adult army, commanded by local councils, residents' associations and traders, engaged weapons more commonly associated with the stress tactics of the US-led war against terror. The introduction of the Mosquito device into public spaces throughout the UK led this charge. The Mosquito emits a noise inaudible to people over the age of (roughly) 25, but that is extremely irritating, and sometimes painful, to those who can hear it. The target of those who use the device is groups of loitering teenagers who are seen as a public nuisance and a deterrent to commerce. In fact, the presence of this device also makes life uncomfortable for adolescents who have perfectly legitimate reasons for being in these areas (including meeting up with friends), as well as smaller (innocent) children shopping with their parents. Despite concerns about negative health effects of the Mosquito and its condemnation by the Children's Commissioner for England,[4] the device, which remains legal, is championed by community leaders who view it as promoting public safety.

While the use of the Mosquito may seem extreme, it is contiguous with more temperate measures routinely employed to curtail teenagers' use of public space with the use of such deterrents as skateboard studs, to lighting,[5] the removal of seating (or steps)[6] and closed-circuit television (CCTV). These passive deterrents, now part of the public landscape, discourage teenagers' participation in the life of the community and further push them to the margins. These instruments of social control don't only affect where kids can hang out, but also shape how we are able to view and experience teenagers. If there are signs that teenagers aren't welcome everywhere we look in public space, then their presence starts to seem inappropriate. Adults notice them and make a mental note to monitor them. Adolescents are increasingly seen as a potential disturbance. Their behaviour and sense of self is affected by this deep-seated prejudice against them in ways that tend, in turn, to reinforce prejudice. Teenagers pass so quickly from being the adored objects of positive attention to unwanted intruders that making sense of this fall from belonging must be confusing and hurtful.

The anxiety provoked by teenagers' presence in public space speaks directly to their status within the community. Public space is idealised as a neutral arena shared by every member of the community, an embodiment of democratic, inclusive values. But what these ideals entail is the subject of considerable contention, in theory and in practice. To be inclusive, we need also to be tolerant of different modes of being, enjoyment and expression that may cause offense or conflict with one's own. Public space, if conceived of as democratic and inclusive, can seem a dangerous and threatening space. This is borne out by the foundation texts of liberal democracy, which take pains to argue the importance of toleration. For the 19th century political philosopher John Stuart Mill, in order to live in free society citizens must be able to express cultural and religious differences. This toleration is to be secured by the 'harm principle', whereby individuals' free expression can only be impeded where their actions trespass against others' life or liberty.[7] Yet public space is always contested space, coopted to and defended against particular interests. The notion of what we should have to tolerate is also controversial. Western citizens are increasingly sensitive to the nuisance created for them by others' enjoyment, so that the extent to which we feel it intrudes upon our own also increases. We feel harmed by others' enjoyment of public space – smoking, playing loud music, preaching, sleeping – and so put pressure on local government and police to move on the offending behaviour.

A new understanding of the purpose of public space, then, is coming to prevail, one that emphasises safety and social control, curtailing freedom of expression for anyone but the perceived majority (middle-class, white adults).[8] Public space, in these terms, is not a place of 'unmediated political interaction' so much as a place of 'order, controlled recreation, and spectacle'.[9] Public space is valued as an arena not so much for the representation of various points of view as for the representation or display of values with which the community is supposed uniformly to identify.

But where order is favoured over inclusion, ambiguity becomes intolerable. Children and adolescents who should be in the private sphere of the home become a social problem. While younger children are viewed as too incompetent and vulnerable to negotiate public space without adult supervision, teenagers are deemed dangerous and unruly, a threat to smaller children and adults alike, and so are barely tolerated in public.[10] Teenagers in public are objects of fear and suspicion, constantly moved on by police and security guards not because they have done anything illegal, but simply due to the anxiety they provoke in adult passers-by.

This anxiety of adults is largely about the in-between, ambiguous zone of adolescence. Many who reminisce about their own juvenile pranks and harmless tomfoolery also demonise the teenagers who hang out on their street corner, attributing to them malignant intentions. Adults read into the presence of loose teenagers a social disorder that threatens communal identity in general and their own safety in particular. Yet adolescents rarely mean to intimidate. Rather, 'threatening' behaviour is only 'a by-product of natural flows of activities' within their own sphere, produced without reference to onlookers.[11] What's threatening about teenagers is not necessarily their actions or any actual interference with others' freedom of movement or expression. Rather, it is their uncertain status that intimidates, their resistance to being categorised as either adult or child: adolescent identity is a work in progress. Through socialising, often pursued in the open, in the safety of public space, teenagers practise who they are. To the extent that such a negotiation is untidy and out of our control, it reveals the uncertainty of adult identity. We alleviate this anxiety by moving them on.

The public space we supposedly share, far from being neutral, is carved up according to geographies of fear and exclusion,[12] a social imaginary that manages adults' vulnerability by limiting the ways teenagers socialise. The struggle for control over public space, epitomised by the use of environmental deterrents to teenage participation, suggests a broader, existential struggle between adults and adolescents, an intergenerational crisis of authority and meaning. One common anxiety about teenagers is that they begin to question their parents' authority and taste, producing different cultural codes through music, social activities and language, thus making themselves impenetrable to adults. Adults often feel confronted and disempowered by these inaccessible meanings and values. French philosopher Jean-Paul Sartre illustrates this crisis in meaning and experience with the apt example of an unexpected encounter in a public park. Sartre describes the familiar situation of walking alone, unself-consciously, in a park. He describes the feeling of comfort and mastery of the person apprehending all they see, imbuing things with meaning and value according to their own experience.[13] 'I', in this instance, am the subject, the one who experiences, and everything else (including other people at a distance) is an object in my world: I apprehend the 'cold-stone' or 'man-reading', for instance.[14] The terrain of the park is, then, organised by virtue of my desires and my experience into one cohesive, sensible world.

Yet for Sartre, at the limits of this experience lies the disintegration of my world. Sartre troubles this happy landscape by introducing another subject onto the scene, one who looks back at me as if *I* were an object and, indeed, with their look, transforms me into an object of their experience, what Sartre calls 'being-for-others'. In this instant, I feel my world drain away, a sudden loss of power, as the world's coordinates are adjusted to the Other's experience, placing them at the centre instead of me. That

I find myself an object of another's judgement, evaluated according to their meaning-giving activities and experience, means that my authority is ceded to another. Sartre's view of intersubjective relations is essentially competitive; his description of social encounters a zero-sum game. There can be no democracy if relationships in public space are conceptualised in these terms.

This manner of experiencing others nonetheless accounts for adults' intolerance of teenagers, who menace us with their enigmatic stares. We experience their presence as a challenge to our values, threatening social change that would topple us from our present positions of authority. Insecurity about teenagers' public presence is reflected in a legal system that is increasingly used as a tool for managing anxiety about youth and anomalous public behaviour, for instance, the UK's Anti-Social Behaviour Order (ASBO) and its Australian corollaries.[15] As well as young people, these legal remedies target others who rupture the homogenous and unchallenging scene of public commercialised space: mentally ill and disabled people, prostitutes and otherwise 'eccentric' individuals.[16] Through the invention of a new normative category – 'anti-social behaviour' – rowdy teenagers are tidied away. As Mary Douglas counsels, if order can be restored, our world and identity will be purified. The very purest social category, innocent childhood, cannot contain the most vulnerable teenagers and nor can adulthood. A place is then created for them within the legal system, managed by law courts, remand centres and probation officers.[17] The community fails to protect these wayward children, and even exposes them to danger. Like baby hippopotamuses they are sacrificed to the ideal of public order.

## Innocence overboard: stateless children

Teenagers are figuratively thrown into the water like hippopotamuses. But in the lead-up to Australia's federal election in 2001, the public was scandalised first, by visuals of boat people jettisoning their children overboard, and second, by the furore that ensued once we found they hadn't, that the whole spectacle was a result of political mischief-making by then Defence Minister Peter Reith. The event, which may have won John Howard a third term as prime minister,[18] was the unfortunate culmination of a tension that had gripped the Australian public between compassion for stateless peoples and a sense of threat by invasion. The presence of children on the *Tampa* complicated the public relations task of framing asylum seekers as nasty queue jumpers and/or terrorists. Reith presented the media with photographs, reputedly of the sea rescue of children thrown overboard by their parents for emotional leverage. The prime minister and other politicians followed with statements to the effect that the *Tampa* refugees were 'not types of people we want integrated in our community, people who throw children overboard'.[19]

Yet after the humanitarian scandal became a political scandal mud continued to stick to the asylum seekers; many Australians still held fast to the idea that these were not the type of people we want around here. The psychological task of framing the refugees was accomplished, the jarring presence of children on the boats neutralised by their having been turfed overboard, if not actually, at least conceptually. And once we were on message that the government saves children, cognitive dissonance was easily assuaged: the shared predicament of children and their demonised parents could be glossed over.

A significant feature of the Australian experience of the global refugee phenomenon is its depoliticisation through a focus on the morality of parenting. The public allowed the government to maintain its hard line on illegal arrivals because refugees were negligent parents. Why else would they pile their kids onto leaky boats? Yet this scandal obscures the fact that children are also refugees. They, too, appeal to international conventions by virtue of being refugees, and not only children. By removing the *Tampa* children from the context of their lived experience, we can see them as transposed middle-class children, as secure from social ills and incapable of independent thought. We can then imagine they are only pawns of their desperate parents.

Another flashpoint of this dissonance between childhood innocence and the predicament of children seeking refuge occurred during riots at Woomera Immigration Detention Centre in 2002. Children participated in hunger strikes and self-mutilation in protest against the length and manner of their processing. The most difficult political action for Australians to fathom was the sewing together of their lips, which many felt was a choice that could only have been imposed upon children, not made by them.[20] According to the kinds of developmental models by which we assess children's competency, they are not capable of weighing up the variables that lead to robust decision making. Yet as was discussed in chapter 4, discourses by which such truths are gleaned themselves emerge from a specific social situation: the nursery, the childcare centre, the school and the reformatory school. These contexts arose from a social movement that took children out of the workplace and sequestered them from ordinary life. Our notions of what children can and cannot do are limited to these cultural milieux. Outside of this context, stateless children perhaps might act politically and have complex ideas and strategies about how best to secure their interests. (It is even possible their parents were sorry to see them negotiate these decisions, and did not hold their children down or deny them food.)

For many Australians, these children were only objects of moral outrage when their parents were accused of abusing them. A small number of advocates battled for their removal from the harmful environment of detention centres. These psychologists, lawyers and other concerned citizens drew strategically on discourses of child development and the emotional capital of the innocent child to argue their case; in a political culture such as ours, no other tactic would have currency.[21] If we could form no sense of common humanity with the refugees as such, perhaps sympathy for their children could be fostered.

Since July 2008, government policy has been that children shall no longer be detained in centres; they are to be housed in community settings along with their families. These children are still captive, however, to a populist bipartisan agenda to politicise refugees. From October 2009 Sri Lankan refugees, including children, have been held behind bars in Indonesia (which, unlike Australia, is not a signatory to the UN convention on refugees), at the behest of the Australian government.[22] Further, in August 2009 Amnesty International reported that 61 children were still being held at the facility on Christmas Island, despite government commitments to the contrary.[23] It seems that this strategy of holding refugees at arm's length satisfies the public. If we look to Mary Douglas' notion of dirt – as matter out of place – it makes sense that the problem of the refugee is at least psychologically resolved by separation. Stateless peoples are liable to provoke anxiety because they have no place. Once children are removed from detention centres, cognitive dissonance is alleviated and anxiety assuaged. We then tend to forget about the conditions beyond our shores that led to their arrival. Politicians and the media have consistently positioned the approach of the leaky vessels in terms of invasion,[24] and the potential burden of asylum seekers on taxpayers, yet perhaps this invasion anxiety masks a more profound anxiety about our presence in Australia and in the region.

The focus of attention on children distracts from the complicated geopolitical and historical factors through which we and the boat people washed up in Australia.[25] These factors are messy and, in the short term, irresolvable. It's tidier to think about the children, who, in their innocence, can be physically and conceptually removed from the geopolitical scene.

## In(ter)ventions of innocence: Aboriginal children

Displaced peoples such as refugees produce confusion, resentment and anxiety because their proper place is uncertain: we only know they do not belong here. The causes of their homelessness seem so remote from the lucky country, the circumstances of their arrival mysterious and opaque. We Australians are 'too innocent' to comprehend the complex and protracted conflicts that lead them here. We, who 'have no history', are impatient with the archaic squabbles of foreigners.

In truth, however, we do have a history and, moreover, a history of homelessness. This continent has long been the resting place of other nations' 'dirt', in Mary Douglas' sense of the word: people out of place. Many convicts were economic refugees, excess population whose poverty was criminalised, just as there were genuine criminals and political reformers. We owe our being here to Britain's need of a spare drawer to tidy its refuse into. Our arrival meant that those already living in Australia were displaced, dispossessed of their land, compelled into homelessness and designated as human dirt.

Between 1869 (*Aboriginal Protection Act 1869* [Cwlth]) and, officially, 1969 (*Aborigines Act 1969* [Cwlth]), Aboriginal children of part-European descent were systematically removed from their families by government agencies. The reasons provided for this measure were framed in paternalistic terms because of perceived neglect indicated by poverty. The chief authorities enacting this policy were named protectors of Aborigines, although there was a demonstrated belief that Indigenous Australians were endangered peoples, cultural and physical throwbacks destined shortly, according to a slapdash Darwinism, to extinction. These protectors were assigned to oversee the gentle demise of full Aborigines (to 'smooth the pillow of a dying race'[26]) and the assimilation of lighter skinned Aboriginal children into the non-Indigenous population. It was hoped that within two or three generations they might even forget who their ancestors were.

No matter how benign these motives may seem to some, in view of the ideological context, evidence of efforts to improve the situation of Indigenous children is lacking. Under this regime, children were physically, sexually and emotionally abused, and frequently consigned to serve as slave labour to their white foster parents or employers (with payment held in inaccessible trusts).[27] Any pretext that the policy served children's interests rather than the imperative to supply cheap labour was compromised in 1915, when the

Aboriginal Protection Act was amended so that the board no longer had to prove neglect before removing children from their family. The following complaint by the colonial secretary illustrates the board's concerns:

> if the aboriginal child happens to be decently clad or apparently looked after, it is very difficult to show that the half-caste or aboriginal child is actually in a neglected condition, and therefore it is impossible to succeed in the court.[28]

The successful removal of Aboriginal children, rather than their protection, was clearly the Act's objective.

What is striking, however, is how committed to the idea of protection those responsible for these policies were. The protectors appear to have believed their own rhetoric, notwithstanding the obvious benefits of the removal policy to the white community. The reality of self-interest was concealed by the discourse of protection. When something is done to another for their own protection, power is wielded under the auspices of beneficence. A lasting good permits temporary cruelty – and these protectors were thinking very long term. A pioneering protector of Aborigines in Western Australia, A. O. Neville, was concerned for a future presaged by the apparently exponential increase of mixed-heritage children. Neville adopted a eugenics-based approach to the 'Aboriginal problem', arguing strongly for the removal and containment of so-called half-castes, quarter-castes and quadroons.

Arguably, non-Indigenous Australians were most anxious about children of mixed parentage because they revealed the extent to which whites could not control themselves sexually. The demand to tidy them away and breed out the colour addressed anxiety not only about where the half-caste belonged, but also the place of Europeans in Australia. If we were not protectors, if we were not the civilised ones, we might be molesters, unable to control our desire. The partially white Aboriginal child showed up this desire as its product, or abject remainder, the part of white Australia we could not bear to acknowledge. Our governments apologised for its manner of dealing with this remainder, but what it means about our belonging here has not been addressed – and in the meantime the language of protection continues to permeate efforts to manage Aboriginal peoples.

As part of the process of reconciliation with first Australians there is an onus to engage with the personal accounts of rebellion and resistance by Aboriginal children, accounts, that is, that complicate our image of them as helpless victims. Such stories are not difficult to find. The autobiographical novel, and then film, *(Follow the) Rabbit-Proof Fence*, for instance, documents the 1931 escape of three removed children from the Moore River Native Settlement back to their family by following 1600 kilometres of fence. Many other stories of resistance are told in *Bringing Them Home*, the report on the Stolen Generations, and *14 Years of Hell*, accounts of the Hay Institution for Girls inmates.[29]

Presently, there are renewed efforts to establish the morally upright position of non-Indigenous Australians, and children are again the focus of this campaign. In June 2007 the Howard government, nominally in response to the Northern Territory government, commissioned the *Little Children Are Sacred* report,[30] thereby announcing its intention to enact radical emergency measures in Northern Territory communities particularly prone to child abuse and neglect. These interventions included such paternalistic protections as banning alcohol and pornography on Aboriginal land, linking income support to school attendance, introducing compulsory health examinations for all Aboriginal children in affected communities, acquisition of townships through five year leases, the abolition of the permit system through which communities had controlled who could access their land, quarantining welfare payments such that a substantial proportion could be spent only at prescribed stores (often hours away from where people live) and, perhaps most controversially, the suspension of the *Racial Discrimination Act 1975* (Cwlth), so the above measures could be enacted. The intervention comes on the back of a long history of policy failure, enacted by socially conservative and progressive governments alike, so it is understandable that Indigenous leaders such as academic Marcia Langton and Noel Pearson should distrust opposition to the intervention from the urban Left. Yet the application of these actions was broad and lacked nuance, affecting individuals who were never suspected of child abuse and reaching deeply into the lives of residents of those communities. Many reported feeling branded by the accusation of molestation, having previously considered themselves upstanding citizens. These actions affect people's daily lives: how they relate to their children and how other people see them.

Parliament gave bipartisan support to the intervention. What politician would question the authority of actions deemed to protect children? There was no space for legitimate criticism of the government response to the report, and critics were hastily accused of callousness towards the children. As is often the case, the intensity of emotional and ideological investment in the sanctity of childhood ('little children are sacred' recalling the cultural significance of children as divine messengers) obscured the detail of public policy. Howard summed up this sense of panic when he compared the situation for Aboriginal children to the effects of Hurricane Katrina,[31] as if it were an emergency that appeared from nowhere rather than the result of two centuries of government ineptitude and underinvestment. Despite the concern for children, which eclipsed concern for women as victims of violence, that justified the intervention; by the time of its one year review no charges had been laid for child abuse. Many Indigenous people suspect that the intervention had more to do with land than children.[32] Given the changes to land tenure and access, and the openings this has created for mining interests, this suspicion may be justified.

In early 2008 the first official duty Kevin Rudd performed as prime minister was to apologise to the Stolen Generations,[33] which Howard had refused to do. The apology was a long-awaited event, and an astute political gesture that earned Rudd considerable praise.

The action drew upon the dense symbolism and emotional cachet of childhood innocence. Rudd continued to deploy this imagery in his statements concerning other issues of public policy. Since the apology the situation of Indigenous people has not substantially altered. What is required is a response that will address people of various locations (rural and urban) and of all ages, because even if for Aboriginal people children are sacred, they are also part of the everyday functioning of their communities.

## Politicising the apolitical child

In each of these cases, a strange equivocation organises our perceptions of children. First, the child is evoked as an irresistible attractor of community concern, the blameless victim we have the power and authority to save, curiously independent of its own community (thus willing to be saved by us). But next, precisely at this point of vulnerability, the child is soiled and so no longer of interest. Repeatedly, the idea of childhood purity is rescued while actual children are scorned.

With the exception of teens, the lives of these fallen children are remote from Australian middle-class experience. It is difficult to imagine middle-class children in the place of Indigenous or refugee children, enacting the kinds of rebellion of which they are capable. But precisely insofar as we perceive children to be essentially apolitical – incapable of political thought and action – they become a potent field through which to manipulate political sympathies against marginalised groups. 'The child' can be used as a political tool only because it is understood to be above politics, which is why actions elicit bipartisan approval once vulnerable childhood is brought into operation.

Suspicion should be aroused when concerned adults advocate children's interests, not because children have no place in politics, but because by invoking the sanctity of childhood, children's opinions and agency are effectively excluded. If we are truly interested in what is best for children, we may need to avail ourselves of the possibility that, for instance, refugee children can engage in radical political action, or that Aboriginal children have complex interests in relation to culture and community. Finally, we might need to confront our fear of teenagers. The next and final chapter will explore childhood and adolescence further, in the context of a reappraisal of representations of children in art and the media.

# Chapter 6

# When fantasies become nightmares

## Purveyors and pornographers of innocence

When the *Bill Henson, 2008* exhibition was locked down by police, debate over his images of naked adolescents polarised between the competing concerns for the protection of children and the freedom of artistic expression. Henson was portrayed by one side as an exploiter of children; by the other he was immortalised as an artist of first merit whose work is above the scrutiny of tabloid-reading philistines.[1] The nature of the discussion meant a middle ground was difficult to occupy. The child-protection camp claimed feelings of uncertainty and vulnerability that many viewers experienced regarding the images. Thus an opportunity was missed to critically reflect upon such feelings and what they say about our ideals of childhood innocence.

Meanwhile, in their failure to address the discomfort provoked by Henson's work, his supporters pushed art to the margins, leaving it to be regarded as an elite field closed to most Australians, which did not engender public sympathy for Henson. Newly elected Prime Minister Rudd had his finger on the pulse of public sentiment when, on breakfast television, he called the most controversial photograph, of a nude 12 year old girl (*Untitled #30*), 'revolting'.[2] It's fair to say that this encounter between the artist, the child-protection activist, the Australian public and the New South Wales police force generated more heat than light. The debate burnt hotly and died out quickly, leaving those involved singed and shy of the public arena. Even the most controversy-hungry artist would baulk at being labelled a child pornographer. Likewise, towards the wane of the affair, Bravehearts campaigner Hetty Johnson reflected on her reputation as a hysterical panic monger.[3] But this encounter was no encounter: once hostilities ran their course, the arts community returned to being aloof, and an indignant public to knowing what they like. No space of exchange was produced, and each party was none the wiser about the other's point of view.[4]

If anything can be learnt from the Henson affair it is that emotions run high where children's innocence is concerned. Children's vulnerability touches us all. This is not only because of biological fragility, that is, their smallness and relative immaturity. As we saw in chapter 5, more is at stake in protecting children than their welfare. Childhood innocence is associated with a host of other Western values, and operates as a proxy for them. The child is emblematic of adults' fragility: we take care of the child as if protecting a part of the self or greater humanity. Adult identity is shaped in relation to the vulnerability of children, as their protectors, and the child represents all that is innocent, vulnerable and, indeed, venerable in humanity itself.

As was suggested in chapter 1, Australians particularly see themselves in the model of the child: as generous, open, egalitarian, as unhindered by the cultural baggage (class, for instance) of the mother country and as essentially innocent. This is why the ANZAC legend came to resonate so strongly with Australians during the Howard years in that it demonstrates our innocence, bravery and

purity of heart in relation to the British, even while ANZAC signi-
fied an identity forming loss of innocence. (Is it incidental that this
reconstruction of Australian innocence took place at a time when
our innocence was most in question, as we were asked to face the
violence of colonisation?)

Outbursts of public sentiment such as those over Henson's exhibition should be read in the context of these lateral issues connected
to feelings about innocence. We could then ask whether the display
of juvenile nudity compromises a child's innocence necessarily. Or
is this equation of nudity and sex a recent sensitivity? If Henson's art
is troubling, how might we give proper consideration to the unsettling effect of his work? Could this effect be productive, or is it
simply indicative of a violation? Would an appreciation of the artistic traditions to which Henson's work refers help us unpick these
concerns? Perhaps what Henson upsets and complicates are conventions of representing childhood innocence we take for granted,
and which give us comfort. Perhaps he upsets a hierarchy of social
agency that requires a narrow construction of childhood as vulnerable yet unharmed, subject to, yet unconscious of, adults' gaze. This
ideal of representation is so precarious that it is inevitable that artists
such as Henson should come to upset the Edenic applecart (provoking questions of agency and sexuality, as does the proverbial snake).

We need also to consider how the viewer is constructed, which is
also a matter of context. *Untitled #30* was received in a media environment that hailed its viewers as protective of the child depicted.
We were bid by Johnson, Rudd and various media outlets to view
the image as parents would. Assuming the role of the parent,
viewers asked themselves if they would allow their child to be
so exposed. Yet as well as being asked to hail the inner parent, we
were also bid to view the image as a paedophile might, to imagine
that, had we visited the Roslyn Oxley9 Gallery, the person standing beside us might have been a child molester. This amounts to a
vicarious identification with the abuser, which, in turn, strengthens
the abject response to Henson's art (as 'revolting'). Viewers' sense
of horror responds to their assumption about the paedophilic gaze.

But in bringing this gaze to the fore, other perspectives are disqualified as potential ways of seeing the photograph. As parents, this should concern us: if the paedophile's perspective comes to dominate, even at the behest of child-protection advocates, childhood increasingly becomes visible only as sexual.

What lies beneath this abject response is, first, a repudiation of sexual desire for children. By viewing the photograph as pornographic we must, despite ourselves, partially identify with that way of seeing the child. The violent response signifies an effort to break away from that identification. But, second, the abject response also indicates an unbidden sense that we might separate children from their innocence by desiring them. This reveals the uncomfortable truth that innocence belongs not to childhood, but adult fantasy. Innocence is a vision of the childhood we feel our children deserve and in which we invest considerable energy because we want to believe in and maintain a life free of desire. If children are deprived of their innocence (meaning there is an incursion of adult material into their enchanted world), we feel complicit in such deprivation. Interpreting our own desire for children under the insufficient rubric of child protection, we unconsciously, guiltily, equate it with sexual abuse.

Yet there is reason to be wary of desire for children apart from the anxiety it provokes about paedophilia. If the vulnerability we want to protect is intrinsic to their value, there is incentive to keep children vulnerable. Conversely, because they are vulnerable – their innocence always at risk – children become society's greatest liability as well as its most precious asset. Incidents such as the Henson affair provide a theatre for the playing out of this anxiety about the importance, and fragility, of innocence.

## Moral panics and their casualties: vulnerability, censorship and consent

Bill Henson has been photographing children for a long time. He is especially interested in adolescence and the ambiguity of the duration individuals negotiate between childhood and adulthood.

Adolescence presents many challenges related to identity and desire. Teenagers receive contradictory signals about what is expected of them and how they should behave. Rarely are these signals positive. They are often depicted by the media as a social menace, responsible for the decay of community. Adults' attitudes towards teenagers are tinged with disappointment about the passing of childhood. As a result, teenagers enter a murky territory induced not only by their own hormones, but also by the cultural feedback they receive about what it means to be adolescent.

A sympathetic viewing of Henson's body of work reveals his sensitivity to teenagers' vulnerability. His photography plays with light and shade, captures the 'twilight' of childhood and the obscurity of the experience of being on the 'cusp of adulthood'.[5] The locations in which he shoots conjure what has been described as 'the secluded gloom of urban wastelands, barren landscapes and 'spellbinding, haunted spaces'.[6] These are the kinds of spaces adolescents like, and often the only places they are tolerated in groups. Henson says that

> intervals in the landscape, the no man's land between one thing and another thing . . . like the vacant lot between the shopping mall and the petrol station is where teenagers . . . naturally go to muck around . . .
>
> Kids naturally gravitate toward that sort of interval in the landscape. I suppose, as we grow older, all those places sort of become a bit of a lost domain.[7]

Because Henson so ably depicts the vulnerability of being adolescent, his work is unsettling. For parents, for whom, especially, the transition from childhood to adolescence is too swift and who often feel ill-equipped for the challenges of adolescence, Henson's images evoke the myriad feelings we have for our children. Using telephoto lenses, he conveys the parent's thwarted, tender protectiveness, exercised from afar (as if we were voyeurs rather than parents, because our children no longer want us near). This parenting at a distance Henson so aptly represents magnifies the sense of fragility we feel towards the subjects of his work.

This vulnerability belongs to the artwork as well as its subjects. And the Henson case demonstrates, the liability to misunderstanding such subtle and profound works suffer out of their proper context. Yet the first removal from context borne by the image was at the hands of the artist himself, who insisted the invitation for the Roslyn Oxley9 opening should feature his most context sensitive and potentially provocative image. In his 'anatomy of a moral panic' *The Henson Case*, David Marr presents the chronology of events that led to the police raids on Henson's exhibition and its aftermath. Marr reveals the uncertainty and ambivalence the invitation provoked:

> The Henson invitation has few friends. I have yet to meet anyone who says they opened the envelope with whole-hearted pleasure. Even those who admired Henson's naked junkies in the 1980s, and didn't flinch from his gawky adolescents in the 1990s partying by night in piles of wrecked cars, were unnerved by the beautiful image of that twelve-year-old child.[8]

Marr, I think rightly, conjectures that the sight of transitional breasts unnerved its viewers:[9]

> Without breasts or with full breasts this image would . . . have caused less fuss . . . But these were budding breasts, rarely seen and almost never celebrated. In our culture budding breasts are extraordinarily private.[10]

The meaning attached to the model's breast buds is that this is a transitory, and so vulnerable, moment of her life. She is in the ambiguous zone of no-longer-not-yet that is hidden from view in our culture because, as Mary Douglas might contend, we're not quite sure how we should categorise it. Early adolescence is an extraordinarily private time, lived behind closed bedroom and bathroom doors, partly because a girl is metamorphosing from child to adult and must come to terms with what that means for her. Perhaps more acutely in terms of public reaction, the budding breast is private because adults do not want to dwell upon the passing of childhood. The budding breast refers obliquely to a budding sexuality and the stirrings of a desire we cannot control.

This reluctance to contemplate the passing of childhood has a lot to do with what is invested in the idea of childhood. If the child is reduced, in the social imagination, to one without worldly experience or desire, a passive object of others' protection, control and abuse, then it is understandably difficult to conceptualise the transition to the activity and knowledge of adulthood. This is especially so concerning sexual activity and knowledge. The apparently radical difference between childhood and adulthood is inflected by other distinctions between immaturity and maturity, dependence and autonomy, and innocence and sin. But what if instead of reducing childhood to innocence, passivity, dependence and ignorance, we considered what kinds of conditions might support the development of the skills children require to negotiate relationships with others? In turn, we might ask: What does maturity owe to immaturity, autonomy to dependence, and adulthood to childhood? Are these categories as opposed in life as they are in language or imagination? Perhaps the incapacity associated with childhood reflects and magnifies a more general feeling of incapacity and helplessness experienced by adults.

I am not suggesting that children and teenagers are not vulnerable. Rather, that adults are also vulnerable and feel especially so in the face of passing childhood, protection over which had afforded them a degree of power and status. As we saw in chapter 5 in relation to Sartre's concept of the look, it is not only the risks faced by adolescents that render us uncomfortable. Adolescents engender the world with their own meanings, values that compete with ours, and which we fail to understand. With the dawning of adolescence, children begin to question adults as authorities. They ignore our good advice, keep secrets and progress more independently. They claim their sexuality and deny legitimacy to ours. What map guides their way, and how will they find us again? Our teenagers turn the tables, leaving us in ignorance, feeling disrespected and impotent. Perhaps most significantly, adolescents seize the field of sexuality and desire to which adults had, in their youth, laid claim. Once children develop into teenagers, sexual desire, desirability and potency rapidly transform (and contaminate) childhood, which tends to be associated with an absence of desire. Teenage desire – and our inability to control it – heightens adults' sense of vulnerability and helplessness, and signals a loss of the sweet refuge from worry and work that childhood innocence is supposed to represent.

The exaggerated conceptual distinction between childhood innocence and adult competence contributes to this fear for children and of adolescence. To move beyond fear and towards more productive ways of coping with adolescents' passage from childhood to adulthood would require an attention to the views of children that is not yet evident in our culture. The PG (Parental Guidance) rating Henson's photograph eventually received[11] underscores this point. The Office of Film and Literature Classification stipulates that items 'classified PG may contain material which some children find confusing or upsetting, and may require the guidance of parents or guardians'.[12] (Although adults seemed to need at least as much guidance as children.) What is needed, then, is an invitation to children to discuss experiences and encounters that assume adult knowledge. The PG rating suggests a more promising mode of relating to children in terms of guidance and a commitment to ongoing discussion, rather than authority and a commitment to protection. Left alone to make sense of something their parents are manifestly uncomfortable about, children inevitably feel confused and upset. Deprived of the resources and relationships that enable an informed engagement with one's environment, anyone would feel that way.

Creating such an opening for discussion means relinquishing our investment in the idea of childhood innocence, understood in terms of ignorance and protection. It also requires re-examining everyday notions of consent and conditions that support human agency.

Consent is usually defined as an individual's capacity to allow another to exercise certain privileges with respect to them. Such consent results from a contract or agreement, and is legitimated by the possession of relevant faculties, such as reason. The one who consents must be able to fully comprehend the range of consequences that issue from their agreement: what is to be gained and lost. We also assume that in order to consent there must be equality between parties; consent is not legitimate if obtained under coercion or duress, where one's capacity to say no is compromised. Children are generally thought not to own such capacity or equality. It is accepted that they have only a partial grasp of their future possibilities and interests and so are easily exploited by others. The view of human nature this notion of consent implies renders children's consent inherently problematic.

Alternatively, we might situate consent intersubjectively, according to very different assumptions about what it is to be a human living in society. We might imagine consent not as a faculty belonging to (complete) individuals, but as a relationship between two or more people grounded in the diverse, unequal, budding capacities of each. This second conception of consent reflects the social condition of human life, a life that requires mutual care and concern. According to this view, 'man' is not an island; rather, all are reciprocally responsible for each other, according to each participant's specific capacities and interests. This conception of humanity emphasises shared dependency over autonomy, but nonetheless promotes freedom of expression and decision. As we saw in chapter 3, Arendt argues such freedoms are only possible because others support them, thereby providing a worldly reception that gives form to individuality. Capacity to consent, according to this framework, is not restricted to fully formed and entirely independent individuals (assuming such could exist); it belongs, rather, to individuals who are limited and enabled by their relationships with others and who in this sense are never fully formed as such, but are formed by reciprocal relations of unceasing change and growth.

In the case of children, this alternative model of consent is a more viable heuristic because it allows for an agency always still in process and so for the participation of children in decision making. By emphasising children's capacities rather than their deficiencies, advanced through relationships with others within a community, this conception of consent provides greater scope for social inclusion. It also places into doubt the naive notion our culture perpetuates: that adults can control the variables that decisions such as consent negotiate. This neglects the limits of adults' decision making, which is always bounded by dependencies upon others and incompleteness of knowledge. Highlighting children's incapacity is a means of deflecting attention from these limits. It supports a conception of adulthood we find reassuring. But the focus upon children's vulnerabilities also prevents an understanding of the conditions under which we all are enabled to be agents, through mutual support and the material availability of choice.

Promoting the conventional account of consent, child-protection advocates were unwilling to concede children might legitimately decide to model for Henson.[13] They held that children – even young adolescents – simply cannot consent, as if this is a capacity mysteriously acquired upon attaining adulthood. This notion of consent refuses children agency absolutely, thereby underestimating their capacity to express unique points of view. Instead of taking seriously the possibility that Henson's model had a legitimate voice, child advocates subjected the parents' decision to scrutiny. At one time or another there were calls for Henson, the parents and the gallery owners to be prosecuted in the interests of protecting the child.

Yet there are good reasons to feel assured that the girl in question did consent. By Marr's account this consent was robust, ascertained over numerous discussions between the artist and the model, the artist and the girl's family, and the family and the model, in which the prospect of future regret was explored and acknowledged.[14] The possibility of such consent was continually doubted throughout the media furore over the image. The budding autonomy of children at this age – their curiosity, experimentalism and independence – disconcerts us. As Henson says in an interview with Marr, in adolescence kids begin to

> go into town on their own, hang out with friends on their own, be no longer attached, absolutely attached, to their parents. I think at about that point there is this remarkable floating world that interests me so much. The potential there is immense, the potential for things to go either this way or that way.[15]

The uneasy arena of potentiality that accompanies making decisions is reminiscent of the fall of Adam and Eve, whose sin was not to pay heed to their Father's prohibition. The risk of making one's own decisions is that things could go awry. Risk is always associated with action, yet no one doubts that this potentiality is valuable, indeed, is what makes us human.

Most agree that having a sense of personal autonomy is key to quality of life for adults, yet the degree to which it is also valuable to children is regularly overlooked. Whether one is active or passive in relation to the events of one's life is a significant determinant of health and happiness. The model's parents took into consideration the broader life context of her decision (that she was starting at a new school and needed a confidence boost, that she loved art, that she had modelled already for her sister's art class) and supported her decision-making process by presenting a range of possible consequences that might arise from that decision. They offered her guidance, but allowed her to decide. In turn, her decision was supported by Henson's respectful behaviour towards her, consistent with his professional philosophy and, by all available accounts, prior practice.

The ensuing expressions of outrage over the photograph were marked, conversely, by disrespect for the girl's decision and a breathtaking lack of awareness of, or concern for, how she might feel about those extreme reactions to her image. Indeed, she was treated as an object. She was a political object, converged on by interests and agendas from both Left and Right. She was a sexual object, displayed in newspapers and screens with salacious black bars across her body. As media researchers Sarah Edge and Gail Baylis write regarding a similar case in the UK, 'This "blacking out" visually confirms, if not actually constructs, the "offensive" nature of the photographs'.[16] The possibility of viewing the image of a child's body as anything other than pornographic is ruled out by the imposition of these visual bleeps.

Finally, Henson's model was an object lesson for Australia's youth, who are liable to be branded 'revolting' by no less than the prime minister if they publically display their agency and vulnerability. Of the numerous opinion pieces published about children's welfare in the midst of the Henson scandal, no one asked for children's opinions. No one treated children as subjects of experience, only as silent, impassive objects. 'What were the parents thinking?' bounced repeatedly around the echo chamber of public opinion. But the question of what the model felt or thought about the fuss made over her body received scant attention.

## Dreams vexed to nightmare: the child in art and advertising

The everyday understanding of childhood is informed by what we see in visual media such as art and advertising. Through very self-conscious practices of representation, these images attach meanings to childhood usually taken for granted because they are conveyed by media that appear not to mediate reality, but, rather, appear to reveal it silently, directly and objectively. We regard the photographic image as somehow more truthful, less creative, than other art forms. The camera neutrally and mechanically captures a slice of reality, so photography is experienced as natural rather than produced. Photography is considered merely a means by which this rather than that moment in domestic experience is quickly and expediently recorded – birthdays, graduations, holidays, any minutiae of existence deemed worthy of preservation.

Invisible to the viewer of the photographic work is a lexicon of symbols and meanings referencing other artistic traditions. Art historian Anne Higonnet puts this well:

> All the visual signs of childhood innocence invented and refined by painting, prints, and illustrations from the eighteenth to the early twentieth centuries were transposed into photography, which rendered them nearly invisible, not because they are not there to be seen, but because photography's reality effect is powerful enough to make the cleverest devices look natural.[17]

With the use of a particular angle of the head, combination of hues, fall of light or flounce of sleeve, the artist cites another work or body of works. The photographic image reads and interprets the artistic corpus as it contributes to it. The artist skilfully manipulates the visual signals through which the work's significance is conveyed. Viewers feel various sentiments – sadness, pride, affection – when viewing art because of an implicit familiarity with cultural conventions of representation. With this visual lexicon and media literacy, the photographer can conjure a perfect exemplar of strength, femininity or innocence, or, conversely, may undercut such ideals and so move us to reflect critically upon them.

If most are more comfortable with older (classic) art than the new, perhaps this is due to art's potential to challenge expectations (an understanding of how the world is ordered). This critical capacity is, however, often abstract and alienating, leading many to dismiss art as useless or even corrosive of the social fabric. The domains of its reception reinforce suspicion that art is an elite preoccupation. As art critic John Berger writes, art is 'preserved in sacred isolation' within museums and galleries 'to which the public at certain hours are admitted as visitors'.[18]

The optics of this separation of art from other forms of visual media played poorly when it came to the Bill Henson affair. The plea for the immunity of art from charges of child pornography worked against the grain of a public that values egalitarianism. It entrenched the notion that there is an elite who consider themselves above public morality, and fed urban legends about esoteric paedophile rings, protected by their place within the professions and the establishment.

The art community, then, fell into a public relations blunder all too familiar to the Australian context: the high/popular culture divide that casts one group as snobs and the other as philistines. The ambiguity of Henson's photograph might have produced a discussion, but instead it invoked a divide between those who feel threatened by its potential meanings and those who are too comfortable with art to experience the productive uncertainty that makes it a critical practice. In this light, the art community missed the point of public anxiety about Henson's work and, as a result, missed an opportunity to reflect upon the social meaning of Henson's art. For this image speaks to everyone, not only an initiated few. It could have also made a positive contribution to current debates about the sexualisation of children.

If we look to philosopher and cultural critic Walter Benjamin, we can take account of the public's negative responses to Henson's images rather than simply discount such views. As Benjamin makes clear, the work of art is meaningful with reference to its critical reception. As surely as hysteria shuts down avenues to appreciating the work of art, so too marginalising a certain kind of response on the basis of its 'lowness' – or its failure to recognise 'real art' – is to deny the work its political and social meaning-giving context.

Written in 1936, Benjamin's 'The Work of Art in the Age of Mechanical Reproduction' responded to an anxiety about the vulgarisation of art through photography and film, as well as his own concern about the Nazis' use of film for propaganda. Benjamin argued that in making art available to the general population, new technologies alter the character of art at its core.[19] After its mass reproduction, the artwork loses its aura, a uniqueness possessed by the work given the specific means of its production, its cultural situation within systems of belief and worldviews, and its material history. Once the artwork can be reproduced, and so viewed out-side its original context, it is opened to multiple interpretations uncontrolled and uncontrollable by the closed sphere for which it was intended. The anxiety suffered by some of Benjamin's contem-poraries was that, with mechanical reproduction, neither the pur-veyors of high culture they saw themselves to be, nor the artist, can control the work's meaning. It is significant for Benjamin that the development of technologies such as the camera occurred alongside the rise of socialism as a political movement: with these develop-ments, art became the province of the masses. This, he argues, 'emancipates the work of art' from its traditional meanings and context – religion, beauty, the concerns of the very privileged and wealthy – so that it comes to serve politics rather than the kinds of unexamined 'ritual'[20] that sustain social inequality. For Benjamin, however, this event of emancipation opens both opportunities and dangers.

Benjamin's mixed feelings about the political effects of mass reproduction are understandable given the uncertain time in which he lived. On the one hand, the liquidation of art – the destruction of its aura to make room for new creative possibilities – signals an involvement of people previously excluded from the reception and production of art, which changes the very nature of art. Where once it had operated at the level of cultic value, embodying a very specific cultural meaning by virtue of its being hidden from view (excepting for those with special privileges), now art operates at the plane of its exhibition. Art is in its being shown, available to anyone who views it, and is now meaningful on the basis of how viewers fit it into their own lives. With the proliferation of the artwork – transported from cathedral to bedroom wall, coffee mug, T-shirt, computer screen – comes the democratisation of art. Such democratisation, for Benjamin, enables art to become a critical practice and its view-ers to be critics of culture and society.

On the other hand, once released to such democratic, critical practice, one of art's dimensions is lost to us (although the nature of this 'us' is precisely what's up for grabs). We can no longer talk of authenticity and specificity. As the mass perspective comes to dominate, the world is flattened, because for Benjamin '[t]he uniqueness of a work of art is inseparable from its being imbedded in the fabric of tradition'.[21] Art can no longer be iconic because it no longer signifies proximity to, or participation in, mystical experience. As art saturates everyday life, it also comes to represent it. Art becomes political and can be a political tool for Joseph Goebbels or any other public figure who deploys images for the purpose of propaganda.

The mechanical reproduction of art, then, reveals that art has no value in itself. It is meaningful only through its frame or context. In earlier times, this frame was its place within the cathedral, court or stately home. More recently, the frame becomes editorial manipulation in the case of the film actor[22] and political manipulation in the case of images of everyday life, invested with significances that inform citizens' experience. In view of the power of representation and the proliferation of images in everyday life criticism is paramount for Benjamin. Without critique, politics itself, along with the consumerism, comes to operate, as does religion, as a life-enframing cult. As every crevice of life is populated by images already invested with political meaning, nothing escapes capture by representation or politics.

In this context, representations of children have come to illustrate a new, apolitical cult or the notion of a humanity that exceeds cynical political and commercial use. Bill Henson's photograph, *Untitled* #30, became a lightening rod for the unease and anger of many that no area of life is sacred, that every aspect of human life is up for grabs, to be consumed by the commercial imperative to consume. The image was received in the context of an ongoing debate about the sexualisation of children by the media, and the concern that even children had come to fulfil an economic function, furthering the expansion of capital. Henson was cast in the same role as Myer or David Jones, as an adult profiting from the bodies of children. The sensitivity aroused by Henson's photograph signalled a dawning consciousness of the increasing use of children's images as avenues to adult desire. The broad rejection of the immunity of art from such criticism was an effect of the democratisation of art, no longer out of reach of ordinary people. Desire is desire, and the appeal to art's separation from the social sphere – to art for art's sake – amounted to a denial of art's political power and resonance with everyday life. Australians were rightly suspicious of the elevation of art beyond politics.

It might then be admitted that Hetty Johnson, Kevin Rudd and other tabloid readers have a stake in the reception of art and a legitimate role in discussion of the meaning of Henson's image, which is political after technologies of mass reproduction. Following Benjamin's insights, there should be a broad critical engagement with commercial and artistic representations of children. Alongside such an interrogation, however, a critical engagement with representations that promote childhood innocence is also needed. Advertisers have always drawn upon art that celebrates childhood innocence, which seems purpose built to sell products. Since Pears' Soap's enormously successful campaigns of the late 19th century (which lately decorate middle-class bathroom walls), advertisers have easily adapted artworks to their own requirements: Millais' *Bubbles*, for instance, which began life as a portrait of the artist's grandson (*A Child's World*) before being renamed and redeployed by Pears', with the strategic addition of a bar of soap in the corner.[23]

That the child could become a privileged subject of art is due to the rapid social and technological changes of the 19th century, changes intimately connected with the rise of capitalism. First, a new middle class conceived of itself as hard working, but also as affluent. Success, in this context, is demonstrated through consumption that augments the household, furnishings that reflect social position but are humble and morally restrained. The mass reproduction of art enabled a proliferation of spaces where art could be displayed. Not only the church or the mansion, but also the walls of the middle-class family home were now covered with famous paintings, thus connecting its inhabitants to aristocratic comfort. This shift in the meaning and purpose of art altered, too, the kinds of things that it made sense to paint. Once art adorned the family home, it could begin to depict these spaces and their occupants, idealising domesticity through the child (and the mother) as a figure of conjugal virtue. In the late 19th and early 20th centuries, as women artists such as Kate Greenaway and Jessie Wilcox Smith found their niche in the art world by depicting children for domestic consumption in magazines and advertising, the representation of childhood innocence was perfected in this social field.[24]

Second, the social changes that led to the proliferation of art and refinement of the notion of childhood innocence through art, also created the conditions in which commercialism could flourish. As the family home came increasingly to represent a place of happiness and comfort, it also became a privileged site of consumption. In the middle-class family home, advertisers found an untapped, virtually bottomless reserve of envy and desire through which they could grab a tenacious hold of our fantasies and wallets. The first condition of commercial success is the gap between identity and desire, between how one sees oneself presently and how one wishes to be in the future. Advertising trades on the sense of lack that comes with (real or imagined) social mobility at the core of capitalist ideology and middle-class identity. As a famous scene from *When Harry Met Sally* illustrates, the belief that 'I' can have (and deserve to have) what 'she' is having motivates consumption. Desire is so associated with what the other has that advertising works by provoking envy and a feeling of deficiency. As Berger puts this, 'the publicity image steals [one's] love of [one]self as [one] is, and offers it back . . . for the price of the product'.[25]

This lack at the heart of consumer desire is connected to the material conditions of everyday life: we go to work and daydream about leisure, in the meantime leaving ourselves barely enough time to feed and water ourselves for the next day's labour. Berger writes that 'the working self envies the consuming self'.[26] And as we saw in chapter 2, our children, who play to compensate us our daily toil, are surrogates for this consuming self. The image of the innocent child propagated by 19th century parlour art and perfected by turn of the century advertising, represents the plenitude and content-ment we all envy and desire. Presented as the centre of family life and flourishing, this image was manipulated by advertisers from the first to stimulate consumer desire by accessing and inciting middle-class aspirations.

Among the most powerful and enduring expressions of child-hood innocence are those found in advertising, from the Pears' ads (depicting naked children reaching precariously for soap), to Cop-pertone (a little girl whose dog is pulling down her bathers, revealing her bare, untanned bottom), to the more recent 'Unworry' promo-tion for insurance (a girl licks icecream to represent a nostalgia for a simpler past, while the voiceover lists things that complicate adults' lives and urges viewers to 'unworry' by purchasing insur-ance). Each of these campaigns trades on childhood innocence to sell commodities. But more than this, each has contributed to the construction of childhood innocence by teaching us that what is most valuable, important and desirable is the innocent child. Child-hood innocence is not naturally separate from the concerns of com-mercialism. Rather, commercialism is the finishing school of the rich, naturalised notion of childhood innocence we currently find ourselves defending from advertising. What's altered since the early days of advertising is that adults have developed qualms about this connection of childhood to consumer desire: the pecuniary inter-ests of advertisers and excessive spending of consumers sullies (and sexualises?) children.

Along with the mass reproduction of art images that heralded the democratisation of art, we have also witnessed the penetra-tion of promotional images in our everyday lives on a previously unparalleled scale. Our experience of the world and of ourselves is saturated by media, which communicate dense information almost instantaneously in a manner that often feels overwhelming. Sensi-tivities about loss of control of our social environment are currently drawn to the issue of the sexualisation of children, who share an adult media environment from which parents attempt to shield them only with great effort. The pace of the media is too fast and it makes us feel passive. In this context, the next generation becomes one more element slipping from our grasp.

Yet if the meaning of childhood is shifting with this tide, and if it looks as if our children might be swept overboard, the best tack may not be an appeal to childhood innocence. For, as I hope is becoming clear, the social investment in childhood innocence produces the conditions through which the sexualisation of children can make sense. The innocent and the sexualised child are part of the same fantasy, albeit a fantasy vexed to nightmare. To establish this connection between innocent and sexualised childhood the shadow aspect of this fantasy will need to be interrogated.

## 'You don't have to be Humbert Humbert... You only have to be a parent'[27]

Advertisements depict desire as lack and offer a product as its solution. The object to which the spectator is drawn, the lure that catches their desire, must be a worthy focus of enjoyment and control, a highly prized possession. Children are today symbols of social value and future security. Their images are drenched with desire. This desire for the child is innocent. It means wanting the best for children: their freedom not to worry about adult concerns and not to be harassed by adult desire, sexual or otherwise. It is fair to say that, as a community, the defence of a desire-free realm, embodied by childhood, has become our highest goal. If we worry about children, it is the incursion of adult desire into their lives that is the most pressing concern.

Yet under scrutiny it becomes evident that this concern to preserve childhood innocence is self-serving and self-defeating, for if our notion of childhood innocence is an adult fantasy produced in response to social changes emerging from the rise of capitalism, then the child is already caught up in adult desire. If the idea of childhood innocence compensates the sacrifices we make daily to 'the man', it cannot be separated from desire. Childhood innocence is the battleground of social anxiety and control precisely because it is so connected to adult identity and desire. Contemporary outrage about the sexualisation of children in the media must be understood in this context. Why are we so agitated by images of children in advertising, when in previous generations even more risqué images were viewed as exemplary of children's innocence? Why is sexualisation seen to be a new trend when children have been on sensual display in advertising from its earliest days? If childhood innocence is in crisis, why now?

One answer to this question might be that the fear of the paedophile lurking in the background of discourse about the sexualisation of children is the guilty product of a rather ordinary desire for childhood innocence. As we saw in chapter 2, some child-protection advocates lobby for government to exert tighter control over the representation of children. An element of this control has been scrutiny of every image of children for its possible sexual allure, through adoption of the paedophile's gaze. Academic and media commentator Catharine Lumby argues that this becomes an exercise in futility once we consider that paedophiles are excited by what most would consider entirely innocent, such as images of the barefoot von Trapp children from *The Sound of Music*.[28] Innocence is the locus of desire for such individuals; looking for signs of a precocious adult sexuality in images of children will always miss the target. That we cannot locate the source of the paedophile's arousal causes even greater anxiety about the control of representations of children, and the scope of what's considered sexual – and even kiddie porn – is ever increasing.[29]

My point, however, is subtly different from this. I do not want to interrogate whether commercial images of children are actually sexual. My interest, rather, is the connection between the fear of sexualisation and the meaning of childhood innocence itself. For what if our fear of the paedophile's gaze indicates a fear of our own desire for children? In other words, the spectre of the paedophile in the background of these discussions of child sexualisation is produced by a fear that we may lose control of our desire. In this light, the ever-present figure of the 'paedophile' (as opposed to actual paedophiles) is our own distorted reflection, just as the sexualised child is the excess of a childhood we fail to control absolutely. A return to the field of art illustrates this idea.

During the Renaissance a revolution in art technique occurred alongside developments in mathematics: the invention of perspective. With perspective, the represented field could be arranged by the viewpoint of the spectator, thus reinforcing their presumed position of control over all within their purview. This trend caught on, and art came to represent social power in other ways too: paintings began to privilege various objects of control, from wives and lovers to cattle, sumptuous food, wine and furnishings, and land. One such painting, Han's Holbein's *The Ambassadors*, depicts two wealthy 16th century adventurers with symbols of *vanitas* resting on a shelf between them, modern instruments of navigation, musical instruments and a bible, symbols of cultural prestige and command.[30] The painting expresses power, accomplishment and vitality. These are Renaissance men, with the world at their feet. Something disturbs the scene, however; in the foreground is a hovering oblong, obscure yet strangely compelling.

When viewed at an acute angle, this blur can be recognised as a human skull.[31] The anamorphic skull is achieved by means of a play on perspective, a bizarre twist upon this new artistic technology that disturbs the viewer's sense of mastery. While perspective is supposed to organise the scene from the standpoint of the spectator and foster a sense of possession over the world it depicts, when plotted to different coordinates the anamorphic object destabilises this control by inserting an alien viewpoint within the image. 'Whatever these men may achieve', it says, 'they are still only mortal.' They will age, may blunder or fall, destitute and alone. This reminder of death undoes their claim to mastery.

As French psychoanalyst Jacques Lacan suggests, the anamorphic 'stain' in our field of vision represents an aspect of the subject's desire that is invested in the world when establishing a relation to it. Almost paradoxically, for Lacan our sense of reality is possible only by means of an imaginative connection to the world through fantasy (such as the social imaginary introduced in chapter 1). Staged in dreams as well as artistic productions, the fantasy articulates the structure of desire. Every encounter with one's environment or with others' is mediated by desire, and desire's aims are revealed in fantasy – for example, the overvaluation of one person and vilification of another. Lacan calls the obscured face of our desire in the object, represented in the painting by the anamorphic skull, 'the gaze'. The gaze stares back at the viewer, but can only be seen from the corner of one's eye as a disturbing, foreign object. The gaze – one's investment in the object – disconcerts because we don't like to admit that how we see the world reflects our desire. But more than this, the skull in *The Ambassadors* represents rogue desire, a piece of the self that, in achieving control over others, escapes our control. Just as a piece of DNA betrays the perfect crime – or a Freudian slip betrays the unconscious intent of the speaker – so the anamorphic foreign object returns to prosecute the guilty self.[32]

We can think of the sexualised child looking back at us from contemporary images, or the paedophile who watches from behind one's shoulder, as such stains on childhood. The paedophile represents the ordinary viewer's excess desire, distorted and persecuting. By directing attention to the paedophile, we can ignore our own investments in, and uses of, childhood innocence. Equally, the sexualised child acts out the aspects of childhood beyond parental authority. It is that uncontrollable element of a field (childhood) that is supposed to be trained to adult desire, as innocent, helpless models of perfected humanity. Both the paedophile and the sexually precocious child are exaggerated threats, rarer than these fears would suggest, which indicates their connection to fantasy. The sexual child and the paedophile are the dark by-products of the ideal of childhood innocence, also a fantasy. The sexualised child only comes into focus once we adopt the ulterior perspective of the paedophile, a perverse and excessive vision that once seen is never expunged. The monstrous allure of the paedophile's gaze is that 'he' can be held responsible for all desire for children, so that the rest can then engage in an apparently unpolluted, innocent relation to children.[33]

The crescendo of fear of sexualisation indicates that the fantasy that childhood purity remains separate from adult life is becoming untenable. With each child who apparently pouts back from a glossy brochure, and thus fails to perform innocent childhood with fidelity, the cognitive dissonances within our desire for children are simply too apparent to tolerate. The cultural fascination with innocent, passive childhood is becoming unseemly, as the question of children's desire and agency emerges as a serious concern. But are these images really more sexual? Or rather could it be that the idea that children might look back so discomfits adults that adults retreat to the notion of childhood innocence in order to avoid it?

## Art, desire and sentimentality

Henson's *Untitled* (#30) confronts us with the child's vulnerability so starkly that its viewers are forced to countenance their own desire for innocent childhood. What they find in this showground mirror is the paedophile. Henson refers to and critiques the conventions of presenting childhood innocence as a lure for adult desire, conventions first forged in art but refined in the earliest, most earnest forms of advertising. The ambivalence and discomfort provoked by the photograph should prompt reflection on the presumed naturalness of these conventions, as well as their precariousness. For the difference between a well-executed, iconic image of innocent childhood and an image prone to charges of pornography is slight. What separates Bill Henson from Anne Geddes is the absence or presence of sentimentality. Sentimentality sugarcoats vulnerability by framing the child in the trimmings of adult supervision. Geddes reassures us of the presence of the adult by surrounding the naked child with citations from nursery rhymes or fairytales, embedding them in adult fantasies of childhood. The spectator of the Geddes image can enjoy the sensuousness of the child's body with impunity because it is mediated by symbols of innocence.

The naked child in Henson's photograph embarrasses our desire for children. If one feels watched by disapproving others while viewing *Untitled* (#30), it is because the photograph is not assimilated into the innocence cult. It allows the viewer no place to hide, does not finesse the desire for youth and beauty. Because Henson's image reveals the viewer's identification with the paedophile (the abject face of desire for the child), it forces either a violent repudiation ('Revolting!') or critical contemplation of the entire field of childhood innocence.

Whatever violence the furore over Henson's exhibition may have done to its intended reception, the reproduction of the photograph in the media opened it to audiences who would never otherwise have seen it. Henson could not control the meaning of his work and had to barricade himself from the media. As Walter Benjamin continues to show us, art is no longer an arcane practice, but is meaningful insofar as it can be criticised. Disappointingly, the productive, democratic potential of such criticism was squandered in the weeks following the release of the image. Enthusiasts on both sides drowned out careful reflection, and there was no room for fence sitters or hesitation through which it might have been possible to explore the visceral response the image provoked.

In an issue of *Art Monthly* that responded to the Henson controversy, artist and teacher Adam Geczy provided a way into understanding the unsettling effect of Henson's image:

> [good] art is always attempting to be 'real'. This real is
> frequently not immediately recognisable because it is not
> a literal or sanctioned transposition of what occurs.
> Paradoxically, this real is a metaphor that actualises and
> divulges the essence of its referent. It can be confrontingly
> hideous, distorted, or so complex as to be embodied in what
> we glean from an abstract form. In the process art has always
> assumed the role of challenging assumed norms of beauty.[34]

Geczy describes the relation Henson's image establishes to the fantasy of childhood innocence. The hideous aspect of the photograph reveals the structure of desire through which reality is established. Thus, it addresses itself to the social imaginary through which our perceptions and possibilities for finding significance are organised.

Those most invested in a discourse of childhood innocence – those who desire innocence to be conceived as a fetishised vulnerability – are violently confronted by what the artwork reveals about this desire. The photograph stages the fantasy of childhood innocence in such a way as to challenge assumed norms of beauty. As did Olive Hoover's beauty pageant performance in *Little Miss Sunshine*, Henson's work forces us to see the concealed eroticism within conventional representations of innocence. If we are to be critical viewers in the manner recommended by Benjamin, this encounter with Henson ought to provoke a renegotiation of the codes according to which values and sentiments are distributed, that is, a questioning of the aesthetic of innocence through which our assumptions about children are communicated. The role of the artist is for this reason *political*, just as beauty and morality are political. And through contemplation of art images such as Henson's, we can begin to imagine what a childhood that thwarts our received notions of beauty – a childhood that is not simply innocent – might look like.

## The crisis of innocence and a new democracy?

In imagining childhood innocence philosophers, artists, writers and politicians have fabricated a weave so dense and complicated that it is difficult to unpick. Its various interwoven patterns are bold, subtle, beautiful and grotesque at turns. The coherence of the motifs of childhood innocence is sometimes elusive, sometimes overwhelming. The innocence of children is so beguiling that at one time or another it seduces the most cynical observers. But that is its problem: we wished upon childhood, imagining it as the last vestige of life free of desire. We closed our eyes and concentrated our highest hopes on innocence and so, investing childhood innocence with desire, despoiled it. Innocence is destined for the corruption of adults' thoughts because it is their creation.

Not everything about childhood innocence is a lie, though: there is a lived world on which the edifices of innocence are constructed. Children often exhibit an openness to others that is admirable, but also terrifying. A truism about children is that they make friends at the drop of a hat, recruiting passers-by – complete strangers – to the games they want to play. They then break these attachments as easily as they were made and wait for the next passer-by. Parents look on with wonder and a sense of fear: if only we could be so easy about relationships. We watch and wait for our children to be hurt by their next encounter.

Innocence is a reaction to the recognition of this vulnerability. It marks an ambivalent moment of recognition, in which positive and negative emotional responses are produced. There are three threads traversing this book that can now be brought together.

1 The vulnerability common to all of us is identified with the innocence of children.

2 Childhood innocence can be a prison, but a selective one: adults police it so carefully that it cannot include all children, and even those who are included are paternalistically excluded from the rest of society.

3 Adults' imaginative retreat into childhood innocence erodes democratic values, favours protection over freedom of expression and reduces democracy's significance to only the freedom of consumer choice.

Resolving these tensions requires an effort to re-imagine our possible responses to vulnerability. Can we re-evaluate vulnerability as a political virtue? What would politics be if vulnerability were distributed more equally instead of gathered into children?

We appreciate children's openness to new people and their inability (reluctance?) to calculate harm. We would like to bottle it, put it on a shelf, measure it out into portions and drink it when required, as if it were a magical elixir. Through the idealisation of childhood innocence this is exactly what we do. But by regulating children's innocence and rendering it inaccessible to others, we annihilate its essential value. What good is openness to others' difference if one's social relationships are strictly controlled? How can children embrace the risk and change they need to develop when wrapped in cottonwool and invested with adults' fear? Innocence is a frozen vulnerability, rendered even more fragile as the child is separated from broader, potentially supportive social networks and so is closed to change and growth.

Perhaps, instead, we could learn something from children, reversing pedagogical and authoritative conventions and the power relations in which they are set. Perhaps we could bring children's openness to others into our social and political field instead of complaining that teenagers, foreigners, homeless people, are taking our resources and destroying our way of life. At issue, then, is how we respond to our own vulnerability. If we choose to take our cues from children, could this lay the path to better democratic praxis (or action)?

What does it mean to revive democracy through the acceptance of human frailty? This recalls the conditions in which modern democracy first came to pass. Democracy was, and remains for many, a wager on which individuals placed their lives at risk. Men and women have been, and continue to be, imprisoned, starved, tortured, raped and killed on the basis of this conviction. There is more at stake for democracy than protection from terrorism or freedom of consumer choice. Australians express pride in our democracy and the strength of the institutions that support it. Yet when refugees, fleeing oppressive regimes, approach our shores in leaky boats, we call them 'illegals' and turn them away or imprison them. Asylum seekers present us with democracy in action by stepping forward to strangers and claiming the rights we take for granted. They enact a vulnerability that makes democracy possible, because if no one had ever asked for rights that were not already theirs – if no one had ever risked their lives for freedom – we would not have a democracy to be proud of. In order to revitalise democratic praxis, then, we need to confront our vulnerability. Presently, the flight from the world of diverse Others into fantasies of childhood innocence and home renovation provides hollow salvation for the precious, world weary, tender subjectivity of the consumer-citizen. It's time to remember what democracy makes possible, and what it opposes.

Those asylum seekers are like children who ask strangers to be their friend. I do not say this to belittle refugees, because there is nothing diminutive about children not already imposed upon them by anxious adults. Children engage in similar struggles for their views to be heard and considered. We can take our cues from children only if we also allow them to participate in our democracy. Otherwise they will remain captive to ideals of innocence, as did Peter Pan or Shirley Temple, innocents who give pleasure as long as they remain in their artificial, miniaturised world. Perhaps our first task in the effort to accept vulnerability, then, should be to solicit children's views in family and community decision making, thus shifting the balance of power so that we are reciprocally vulnerable to them. There are two principles that can guide our way.

First, we must accept that adults are not naturally in less need of protection than are children. Political and legal institutions under-write our safety, just as the family supposedly guarantees children's protection. This is most obvious where protection is removed. When others refuse to recognise our human rights or citizenship, we are rendered vulnerable and powerless, an imminent possibil-ity whenever we travel overseas. We are vulnerable also to an increasingly unpredictable natural environment that does not recog-nise treaties or conventions. Geopolitics and global warming dwarf adults, yet children are defined by their vulnerability. Concern for children's protection eclipses their right to free expression. Not only do children's expressions remain unrecognised, but we also find them threatening (see chapters 5 and 6).

Second, we must accept that children are no less aware of their needs and desires than are adults theirs. Children are largely excluded from democratic institutions because adults presume to better understand their true interests. But how can this assumption be tested if there are no avenues for children to register their claims? Paternalism's flaw must be recognised in the case of children, just as it must in relation to Aboriginal governance. Consigning chil-dren to the status of mere adults in waiting, or not-yet-citizens, silences their views of their own situations. Supporting children's participation through adult political institutions enables their ideas to emerge and develop, and situates this development in a space where intergenerational understanding becomes central. Once included in a democratic process, we may find that children rise to the occasion, their decision-making capacities strengthened by the structural support adults take for granted. Adults, too, become aware of their desires, needs and identities through the social interactions and institutionally mediated practices that comprise democracy. How can we resolve in advance that children haven't the capacity to understand their own needs if we exclude them from the social processes through which our needs and desires are disclosed?

This process of ceding authority and opening to Otherness culminates in taking responsibility. Adults already imagine themselves as the responsible ones. Our mandate to protect children is couched in the language of responsibility, and in protecting children we see ourselves as taking responsibility for their frailty. But if we look back through the looking glass, through the fantasy of childhood innocence that organises these perceptions, we find children taking responsibility for our vulnerability by playing the part of humanity's infinite fragility. What would transpire if we were to take responsibility for our fantasies of childhood innocence? What if we were to recognise our stake in this sequestered childhood as the site of human vulnerability overall? Could this form the basis of a new social contract for intergenerationally and interculturally re-imaging social relationships?

The crisis of childhood innocence presents an opportunity to reconsider political society and snatch it back from consumer capitalism, for which the child is the ultimate desire object. There are two ways we could go from here: we could reinvest in innocence, as Hamilton, Devine and other media commentators and politicians demand, or we could perform a thoroughgoing cultural critique of the importance of innocence to political community. If an equitable distribution of vulnerability is our goal, we must take the second option.

# Notes

### Chapter 1: Why do we worry about children?

1　See Patton et al., 'Global Patterns of Mortality in Young People', for a summary of this research; see the Murdoch Children's Research Institute's coverage, accessed at www.mcri.edu.au/pages/research/news/2009/9/teens-and-young-adults-most-at-risk-of-death.asp, 16 October 2009.

2　Richard White, *Inventing Australia: Images and Identity 1688–1980*, Sydney: Allen & Unwin, 1981.

3　See also Alison Bashford's *Imperial Hygiene: A Critical History of Colonialism, Nationalism and Public Health*, New York: Palgrave MacMillan, 2004.

4　White, *Inventing Australia*, p. 121.

5　Peter Pierce, *The Country of Lost Children: An Australian Anxiety*, Melbourne: Cambridge University Press, 1999.

6　Synecdoche is a figure of speech that represents a whole as one of its parts ('the crown' for 'the monarch', or '20 sails' for '20 ships') or a part by the more general term ('cat' for 'lion' or 'steel' for 'sword'). It is often used in political rhetoric to engender emotional response and to reduce or enlarge the scope of a problem; see D. Stone, *Policy Paradox: The Art of Political Decision Making*, London and New York: W. W. Norton, 1997.

7　Abstinence-only sex education is a feature of the US school system that has recently begun to infiltrate Australian schools. Accessed at www.smh.com.au/national/todays-lesson-condoms-in-the-classroom-cause-controversy-20091202-k6fc.htm, 9 December 2009; see also A. E. Doan and J. C. Williams, *The Politics of Virginity: Abstinence in Sex Education*, Westport: Praeger, 2008.

8　See www.smh.com.au/lifestyle/lifematters/smack-the-child-go-to-jail-parents-pressured-20090822-euef.html. Former Prime Minister Rudd also weighed in on the issue; accessed at www.smh.com.au/national/youve-got-to-be-cruel-to-be-kind-says-pm-20091016-h1cp.html, 21 October 2009. The Australian novel *The Slap* (Christos Tsiolkas), which has received a lot of attention, also works through contemporary ambivalences about smacking.

9　While the concept of social imaginary was developed by Cornelius Castoriadis, it contributes to a tradition that also includes psychoanalyst Jacques Lacan, French feminists Michèle Le Doeuff and Luce Irigaray, Canadian philosopher Charles Taylor and the Australian philosopher Moira Gatens.

10　See www.treasurer.gov.au/DisplayDocs.aspx?pageID=&doc=transcripts/2006/133.htm&min=phc, accessed 16 October 2009.

11　See www.dailytelegraph.com.au/news/nsw-act/no-kids-julia-unfit-to-lead-heffernan/story-e6freuzi-1111113453564, accessed 11 June 2010. Gillard had earlier been criticised by the media because photos of her kitchen for a *Women's Weekly* feature included an empty fruit bowl.

12　Admittedly, the increase was also precipitated by the baby bonus (see chapter 4). This sum by no means compensated the cost of caring for a child and so cannot explain away the effects of imaginary cultural value.

### Chapter 2: Consuming the innocent: Innocence as a cultural and political product

1　Industry officials quote $5 billion as the figure; see James Kincaid, *Erotic Innocence: The Culture of Child Molesting*, Durham and London: Duke University Press, 1998,

p. 103. There is no equivalent in Australia, although shopping centres regularly host baby contests sponsored by companies marketing baby products. The first pageant in the UK, the Miss & Mr British Isles contest, was reported in the British press as 'crass' and 'American'; accessed at www.dailymail.co.uk/femail/article-1032029/Mummys-little-Lolita-The-11-year-old-girl-beauty-treatments-cost-300-month-make-look-like-Barbie.html, 12 February 2009.

2     The Ramsey case is notable for its longevity and the excessive amount of media attention it received. There are still websites and around 1800 YouTube videos dedicated to JonBenét. The case was reopened in February 2009; accessed at www.coloradodaily.com/ci_13112748#axzz0v1qlVYWL, 29 July 2010.

3     E. Rush and A. La Nauze, 'Corporate Paedophilia: Sexualisation of Children in Australia', discussion paper no. 90, October 2006, The Australia Institute: pp. ix, 44.

4     Other recommendations include commissioning a longitudinal study into 'the effects of premature and inappropriate sexualisation of children' (Recommendation 2, 3.30, v), and that state and territory governments introduce comprehensive sexual health and relationships education programs into schools that would include parents and young people (Recommendation 13, 6.39, vii). Thus, the committee farmed out responsibility to bodies other than the federal government.

5     See in particular Lumby and Albury, 'Too much? Too young? The sexualisation of children debate in Australia', *Media International Australia*, Special Issue: 'Children, Young People, Sexuality and the Media', 135 (2010), pp. 141–52.

6     Accessed at www.tai.org.au, 30 January 2009.

7     On this point I am sympathetic to Alan McKee's view in his article 'Everything is Child Abuse', *Media International Australia*, Special Issue: 'Children, Young People, Sexuality and the Media', 135, May 2010, pp. 131–40.

8     Ironically, too, nostalgia for adults' lost youth is now the hottest new thing, as marketers target preconscious consumer desires by repackaging childhood memories such as those of *The A-Team*, the 2010 film version of which the original star, B. A. Baracus, found too sexual and violent.

9     *Corporate Paedophilia*, figure 5, p. 9.

10    Accessed at http://news.theage.com.au/breaking-news-national/obesity-epidemic-now-affecting-babies-20090207-804u.html, 29 July 2010.

11    See T. Veblen, *The Theory of the Leisure Class*, Oxford and New York: Oxford University Press, 2007.

12    V. A. Zelizer, *Pricing the Priceless Child: The Changing Social Value of Children*, New York: Basic Books, 1985.

13    J. Qvortrup argues, contra Zelizer, that schooling is not a withdrawal of children's labour from the system of production, but rather, that we underestimate the work that children perform at school and should factor it into domestic product instead of viewing children as a drain on resources; see Qvortrup, 'From Useful to Useful: The Historical Continuity of Children's Constructive Participation', *Sociological Studies of Children*, 7, 1995, pp. 49–76.

14    Whereas many see school as children's safe haven from society, it is also arguable that broader social inequalities are simply reproduced within the school and that the educational setting is simply a microcosm of society. See Connell et al. on the reproduction thesis, *Making the Difference: Schools, Families and Social Division* (Sydney: Allen & Unwin, 1982); see also Rose, 'Peter Pan, Language and the State: Captain Hook Goes to Eton', in *The Case of Peter Pan or The Impossibility of Children's Fiction*, London: Macmillan, 1984, pp. 115–36.

15    G. P. Stone. 'The Play of Little Children', *Quest*, 4(1), 1965, pp. 25–6.

16    Ibid., p. 24; P. Ariès, *Centuries of Childhood*, Ringwood: Penguin Books, 1973, pp. 61–97.

17 In Marx, surplus value refers to the difference between what a labourer is paid and the value of that labour to the employer; productivity must exceed the cost of hiring in order to generate the surplus, which is the profit. Such profit generation is what constitutes the capitalist system; see Marx, *Critique of Political Economy*; accessed at www.marxists.org/archive/marx/works/1859/critique-pol-economy/ch01a.htm, 18 February 2009. Culturally, play is the surplus value of our labour, hence the child's fetish value. The child represents the profit and significance of our labour.

18 Zelizer, *Pricing the Priceless Child*, chapters 2–3.

19 P. D. Norton. 'Street Rivals: Jaywalking and the Invention of the Motor Age Street', *Technology and Culture*, 48, April 2007, pp. 331–59; see also *Fighting Traffic: The Dawn of the Motor Age in the American City*, Cambridge, MA: The MIT Press, 2008.

20 Accessed at www.abc.net.au/rn/rearvision/stories/2009/2449914.htm, 13 February 2009.

21 Stone, 'The Play of Little Children', p. 24.

22 M. M. Bakhtin, *Rabelais and His World*, trans. H. Iswolsky, Bloomington: Indiana University Press, (1965) 1980.

23 G. Agamben, *Profanations*, trans. Jeff Fort, Brooklyn: Zone Books, 2007, p. 73.

24 The tone Adams uses in the paragraphs preceding this one is even stronger; accessed at www.youngmedia.org.au/whatsnew/archive/adams_paedophiliainc.htm, 19 February 2009.

25 J. Gale. 'The Sexualisation of Children', *Unleashed*, ABC *Online*, 3 March 2008. Notably, the research Gale mentions here is not referenced, and her evidence is the Australia Institute reports, at best a statement of opinion, with no significant or well-evidenced research to back them. Substantial evidence-based research linking exposure to sex ads and other sexualised paraphernalia is lacking.

26 A. Quart, *Branded: The Buying and Selling of Teenagers*, Cambridge, MA: Perseus, 2003, pp. 17–35.

27 Kincaid, *Erotic Innocence*, p. 14.

28 Y. Stavrakakis, *The Lacanian Left: Psychoanalysis, Theory, Politics*, Edinburgh: Edinburgh University Press, 2007, p. 228.

## Chapter 3: The communal fantasy and its discontents: The child's place in political community

1 J. Howard, 'To Stabilise and Protect', address to the Sydney Institute, 25 June 2007.

2 L. Althusser, 'Ideology and Ideological State Apparatuses', *Lenin and Philosophy and Other Essays*, trans. Ben Brewster, London: New Left Books, 1971, p. 164; emphasis in the original.

3 J. L. Austin, *How To Do Things With Words*, Oxford: Clarendon Press, 1962.

4 R. Kipling, 'The White Man's Burden'. This poem refers to the coloniser's patronising sense of obligation to the cultural development of those whom they displace and dispossess. It is the mantle of respectability and nobility that thinly conceals the many benefits Europeans derived from colonisation.

5 R. Bottigheimer, 'The Child-Reader of Children's Bibles, 1656–1753', in Elizabeth Goodenough, Mark A. Heberle and Naomi Sokoloff (eds), *Infant Tongues: The Voice of the Child in Literature*, Detroit: Wayne State University Press, 1994.

6 '*Les rêveries du promeneur solitaire*', quoted in J. C. Steward, *The New Child: British Art and the Origins of Modern Childhood, 1730–1830*, Seattle: University Art Museum and University of Washington Press, 1995, p. 15.

7 Locke published, in 1693, *Some Thoughts on Education*, which strongly influenced Rousseau's *Émile: or, on Education* (1762).

8    J.-J. Rousseau, *Émile*, trans. Barbara Foxley, London and Melbourne: Everyman's Library, 1974, p. 1.

9    Rousseau fathered five children to his lover, Thérèse Levasseur. Each child was placed in a foundlings' hospital, which, at that time, was tantamount to a sentence to lifelong poverty, if not death.

10   The education of women is outlined in Book V of *Émile*. Unsurprisingly, it received a negative reception from feminist political philosophers of the time, most notably Mary Wollstonecraft, who devoted a chapter in her *A Vindication of the Rights of Woman* to a reply to Rousseau.

11   J. Rawls, *A Theory of Justice*, Cambridge, MA: Belknap Press of Harvard University Press, 1971, p. 137.

12   Ibid., p. 250.

13   Ibid., pp. 248–9.

14   Ibid., pp. 128–9. This is compatible with Rawls' principle of paternalism and apparently ensures the care of interests of other generations.

## Chapter 4: Disciplining innocence: Knowledge, power and the contemporary child

1    M. Foucault, *History of Sexuality: Volume I: An Introduction*, trans. Robert Hurley, Ringwood: Penguin Books, 1990, pp. 138; emphases in the original.

2    M. Foucault, *Discipline and Punish: The Birth of the Prison*, trans. Alan Sheridan, New York: Vintage Books, 1979.

3    M. Foucault, *History of Sexuality*, p. 30.

4    J. Rose, *The Case of Peter Pan or The Impossibility of Children's Fiction*, London: Macmillan, 1984.

5    Prior to about the 18th century, 'family' referred to a household not necessarily related by blood. Employees were considered family as much as biological children were, including children in Europe who were usually apprenticed to other households around the age of eight or nine; see S. Jackson, 'Understanding Everyday Experience', in Laurie Taylor (ed.), *Childhood and Sexuality*, Oxford: Basil Blackwell, 1982, pp. 32–8.

6    The internet has increased the capacity to monitor and rank children through sites such as www.babycenter.com, which sends a weekly update (from gestation) to parents informing them what their baby should be doing at this stage of their short existence; accessed 16 November 2009.

7    R. Guest, 'The Baby Bonus: A Dubious Policy Initiative', *Policy*, 23(1), 2007, p. 11.

8    Ibid., p. 13.

9    Accessed at www.theage.com.au/news/national/baby-bonus-a-health-risk-doctors/2007/11/08/1194329414514.html, 11 November 2009.

10   Evidence suggests that pronatalist inducements alter the timing of childbirth rather than its frequency, and so do not substantially affect population in the longer term; see Guest, 'The Baby Bonus', pp. 13–14.

11   Accessed at www.smh.com.au/world/balloon-boy-hoax-fears-after-falcon-says-we-did-this-for-the-show-20091016-h0j8.html, 14 November 2009.

12   Shows such as *The Brady Bunch*, *Different Strokes*, *Family Ties*, etc., occasionally dealt with special challenging topics, but the default position of the family was that it was well functioning and problems were easily absorbed by the end of an episode. The new trend is that the default point is a vaguely uncomfortable and insurmountable dysfunction that is, nonetheless, good enough for family members to stay together.

13  N. Frost and M. Stein, *The Politics of Child Welfare: Inequality, Power and Change*, New York and London: Harvester Wheatsheaf, 1989, p. 27.

14  See especially A. E. Manning, *The Bodgie: A Study in Psychological Abnormality*, Sydney: Angus & Robertson, 1958; see also J. Stratton, 'Bodgies and Widgies – Youth Cultures in the 1950s', *Journal of Australian Studies*, 8(15), 1984, pp. 10–24.

15  For instance, until 1972, the province of Alberta, Canada, engaged in eugenic sterilisation of children who officials deemed to be slow witted; accessed at www.whatsorts.net/ideas.htm, 9 November 2009.

16  These sciences sought signs of degeneracy in children first on the visible body surface (bumps and ridges, ticks and mannerisms) and later, through the development of intelligence testing, on the soul. N. Rose, *Governing the Soul: The Shaping of The Private Self*, London and New York: Routledge, 1990, pp. 132–50; see also A. Turmel, *The Historical Sociology of Childhood: Developing Thinking, Categorization and Graphic Visualization*, Cambridge: Cambridge University Press, 2008.

17  Foucault, *History of Sexuality*, pp. 27–32.

18  S. Freud. 'Three Essays on the Theory of Sexuality', in Angela Richards (ed.), *On Sexuality*, The Penguin Freud Library, vol. 7, trans. James Strachey, Harmondsworth: Penguin Books, 1977, p. 88.

19  Freud referred to the principle of recapitulation in 'Three Essays' (p. 40); it is also assumed by the argument he presents for the analogy between children and primitive peoples in *Totem and Taboo*, trans. A. A. Brill, New York: Moffat, Yard & Co., 1918.

20  John Bowlby and Donald Winnicott are best known for their developments of attachment theory, or theories about infants' need for intimacy with the mother; see also N. Rose, *Governing the Soul*, London: Routledge, 1989, and D. Riley, *War in the Nursery: Theories of the Child and the Mother*, London: Virago Press, 1983.

21  Wilfred Bion theorised the child's need to have their emotional distress contained by their mother; see W. Bion, 'Attacks on Linking', in W. Bion (ed.), *Second Thoughts: Selected Papers on Psycho-Analysis*, London: Karnac Books, 1967.

22  A. Quart, *Hothouse Kids: The Dilemma of the Gifted Child*, New York: Penguin Books, 2006.

23  F. W. Cline and J. Fay, *Parenting with Love and Logic: Teaching Children Responsibility*, Colorado Springs: Pinon Press, 1990.

24  C. F. Levander, *Cradle of Liberty: Race, the Child, and National Belonging from Thomas Jefferson to W. E. B. Du Bois*, Durham and London: Duke University Press, 2006, p. 7.

### Chapter 5: Fallen innocents: Adolescents, Aboriginal and stateless children

1  M. Douglas, *Purity and Danger: An Analysis of the Concepts of Pollution and Taboo*, London and New York: Routledge Classics, 2002, p. 3.

2  Ibid., pp. 44, 2.

3  Douglas is referring here to a study by E. E. Evans-Pritchard; Ibid., p. 49.

4  See www.childrenscommissioner.gov.uk/content/press_release/content_335, accessed 2 August 2010.

5  As a deterrent to teenagers, a residents' association in Nottinghamshire has installed pink lighting that shows up acne; see http://news.bbc.co.uk/2/hi/uk_news/england/nottinghamshire/7963347.stm, accessed 22 June 2009.

6  A Surrey local council spent £15 000 reconstructing three steps because, according to a local councillor, they were 'like ready-made seats so changes will be made to make the area less attractive to young'; see www.yourlocalguardian.co.uk/news/2272425.taking_steps_to_deter_kids_having_a_sitdown_in_rosehill/, accessed 22 June 2009.

7   J. S. Mill, *On Liberty and Other Writings*, Stefan Collini (ed.), Cambridge: Cambridge University Press, 1989, p. 109.

8   For an Australian angle on the politics of public space, see Ghassan Hage's *White Nation: Fantasies of White Supremacy in a Multicultural Society*, Sydney: Pluto Press, 1998; see also Hage, *Against Paranoid Nationalism: Searching for Hope in a Shrinking Society*, Sydney: Pluto Press, 2003.

9   D. Mitchell, 'The End of Public Space? People's Park, Definitions of the Public, and Democracy', *Annals of the Association of American Geographers*, 85(1), 1995, p. 125.

10  G. Valentine, *Public Space and the Culture of Childhood*, Aldershot: Ashgate, 2004.

11  Ibid., p. 87.

12  D. Sibley, *Geographies of Exclusion*, London and New York: Routledge, 1995.

13  J.-P. Sartre, *Being and Nothingness: An Essay on Phenomenological Ontology*, trans. Hazel E. Barnes, London and New York: Routledge, 2003, p. 279.

14  Ibid., p. 280.

15  See the New South Wales Bail Amendment Bill (2007) at www.parliament.nsw.gov. au/prod/parlment/nswbills.nsf/d2117e6bba4ab3ebca256e68000a0ae2/ 6bf2f2486ad8d397ca257376001cf9b6?OpenDocument. This is discussed on *Background Briefing*, 'Hoons and Young Troublemakers', 7 September 2008; accessed at www.abc. net.au/rn/backgroundbriefing/stories/2008/2353118.htm; see also interview with Michael Atkinson on *Stateline*, 24 August 2007, accessed at www.abc.net.au/stateline/ sa/content/2006/s2015871.htm. A South Australian parliamentary delegation traveled to the UK in April 2008 to learn about how ASBOs are administrated; see www.parliament.sa.gov.au/LegislativeCouncil/Members/Travel%20Reports/ HoodUKPolandTurkey08Report8a.pdf, accessed 2 August 2010.

16  Hewitt, 'Bovvered?'; Matt Foot, 'A triumph of hearsay and hysteria: Asbos are targeting the vulnerable so the government can win votes', *Guardian*, accessed at www.guardian. co.uk/politics/2005/apr/05/ukcrime.prisonsandprobation; see also the BBC *News Magazine* 'Asbowatch' series, starting at http://news.bbc.co.uk/2/hi/uk_news/magazine/ 3674430.stm, accessed 2 July 2009.

17  There is, however, variation in approaches to youth and the law between the states and territories. For instance, Victoria is generally more progressive (making use of diversionary programs in preference to incarceration) than New South Wales or South Australia.

18  D. Marr and M. Wilkinson, *Dark Victory: How a Government Lied Its Way to Political Triumph*, Sydney: Allen & Unwin, 2004; R. Devetak, 'In Fear of Refugees: The Politics of Border Protection in Australia', *International Journal of Human Rights*, 8(1), Spring 2004, pp. 101–9; A. Burke, *In Fear of Security: Australia's Invasion Anxiety*, Melbourne and Cambridge: Cambridge University Press, 2008.

19  Accessed at http://phorums.com.au/archive/index.php/t-60266.html, 20 November 2009.

20  This response is interesting when considered alongside moral panics about self-harm (cutting) among middle-class teenage girls. This is most often pathologised or used as ammunition against raunch culture, but is never considered as political expression.

21  The organisation ChilOut consistently focused on the presence of children to achieve better outcomes for refugees; see www.chilout.org/, accessed 21 November 2009.

22  See http://news.smh.com.au/breaking-news-national/pm-broke-word-over-asylum-seekers-libs-20091120-ipyc.html, accessed 21 November 2009.

23  'Government response to report on immigration detention unacceptable', accessed at www.amnesty.org.au/news/comments/21567/, 2 August 2010.

24    See A. Burke, *In Fear of Security: Australia's Invasion Anxiety*, Melbourne and Cambridge: Cambridge University Press, 2008.

25    T. Nicolacopoulos and G. Vassilacopoulos, 'Racism, Foreigner Communities and the Ontopathology of White Australian Subjectivity', in Aileen Moreton-Robinson (ed.), *Whitening Race*, Canberra: Aboriginal Studies Press, 2004, pp, 32–47.

26    The expression was coined by the anthropologist and humanitarian Daisy Bates in *The Passing of the Aborigines: A Lifetime Spent Among The Natives Of Australia*, London: Murray, 1938.

27    Senate Inquiry in Stolen Wages, accessed at www.aph.gov.au/Senate/committee/legcon_ctte/stolen_wages/index.htm, 7 December 2009; see also R. Kidd, *Hard Labour, Stolen Wages: National Report on Stolen Wages*, Sydney: Australians for Native Title and Reconciliation, 2007.

28    As quoted in the New South Wales Government Submission to the National Inquiry into the Separation of Aboriginal and Torres Strait Islander Children from Their Families, *Securing the Truth*, p. 44.

29    D. Pilkington, *Follow the Rabbit-Proof Fence*, St Lucia: University of Queensland Press, 1996; B. Djuric, *14 Years of Hell: An Anthology of the Hay Girls Institution 1961–1974*, Hay: Women About Hay, 2008.

30    R. Wild and P. Anderson, *Ampe Akelyernemane Meke Mekarle (Little Children Are Sacred)*, report of the Northern Territory Board of Inquiry into the Protection of Aboriginal Children from Sexual Abuse (2007). As Sarah Maddison points out in *Black Politics: Inside the Complexity of Aboriginal Political Culture* (Sydney: Allen & Unwin, 2009, p. 15), the authors 'were devastated that their report had been used to justify the intervention'.

31    Howard, 'To Stabilise and Protect', p. 3.

32    Pat Turner, former head of ATSIC, expressed this view; quoted in R. Stringer, 'A Nightmare of the Neocolonial Kind: Politics of Suffering in Howard's Northern Territory Intervention', *borderlands e-journal*, 6(2), (2007), accessed at www.borderlands.net. au/vol6no2_2007/stringer_intervention.htm, 2 August 2010.

33    'Apology to Australia's Indigenous Peoples', 13 February 2008, accessed at www.pm. gov.au/node/5952, 8 December 2009.

## Chapter 6: When fantasies become nightmares: Purveyors and pornographers of innocence

1    The Australia Council writes: 'Bill Henson is widely recognised as one of Australia's foremost visual artists, with a stellar international reputation, and his full body of work should be viewed in this context'; accessed at www.australiacouncil.gov.au/news/news_items/australia_council_comments_on_bill_henson_affair, 22 April 2009.

2    See www.smh.com.au/news/arts/nude-photographs-revolting-rudd/2008/05/23/1211183044543.html, accessed 23 April 2009.

3    See www.abc.net.au/tv/fora/stories/2008/06/26/2286735.htm, accessed 22 April 2009.

4    Since this chapter was written, Kate MacNeill published an article that also addresses this failure of communication and, more particularly, the failure of the art media to face up to the question of what happens to the image out of context once its meaning is no longer bounded by the art system that credentials art; see 'When Subject Becomes Object: Nakedness, art and the public sphere', *Media International Australia*, Special Issue: 'Children, Young People, Sexuality and the Media', 135, May 2010, pp. 82–93.

5    See text for his *Twilight: Photography in The Magic Hour* collection at Victoria and Albert Museum at www.vam.ac.uk/collections/photography/past_exhns/twilight/henson/index. html, accessed 20 April 2009.

6    See www.pavementmagazine.com/billhenson.html, accessed 20 May 2009.

7   Quoted in D. Sidhu, 'Nocturne: The Photographs of Bill Henson', *Ego Magazine*, August 2005.

8   Ibid., p. 4.

9   Miranda Devine briefly refers to the model's 'budding breasts of puberty' in her first missive, 'Moral Backlash Over Sexing Up of Our Children', published the day of the exhibition's opening; accessed at www.smh.com.au/opinion/moral-backlash-over-sexing-up-of-our-children-20080521–2gts.html, 29 May 2009.

10   D. Marr, *The Henson Case*, Melbourne: Text Publishing, 2008, p. 5.

11   Marr reported at the time that 'The classifiers found the "image of breast nudity . . . creates a viewing impact that is mild and justified by context . . . and is not sexualised to any degree" '; accessed at www.smh.com.au/news/arts/henson-photo-not-porn/2008/06/05/1212259014096.html, 27 May 2009.

12   Cited by Young Media Australia, accessed at www.youngmedia.org.au/codes/classifications_films.htm, 27 May 2009.

13   For further discussion of the tension between the protection of children and their right to decide, see k. valentine, 'Innocence defiled, again? The art of Bill Henson and the welfare of children', *Australian Review of Public Affairs*, June 2008.

14   Marr, *The Henson Case*, pp. 108–11.

15   Ibid., p. 34.

16   S. Edge and G. Baylis, 'Photographing Children: The Works of Tierney Gearon and Sally Mann', *Visual Culture in Britain* 5(1), Summer 2004, p. 76.

17   A. Higonnet, *Pictures of Innocence: The History and Crisis of the Ideal Childhood*, London: Thames and Hudson, 1998, p. 73.

18   J. Berger, 'Understanding a Photograph', in Alan Trachtenberg (ed.), *Classic Essays on Photography*, New Haven: Leete's Island Books, 1980, p. 291.

19   W. Benjamin, 'The Work of Art in the Age of Mechanical Reproduction', in *Illuminations*, trans. Harry Zohn, New York: Schocken Books, 1968, §VII, p. 227.

20   Ibid., §IV, p. 224.

21   Ibid., p. 223.

22   Ibid., §IX, p. 230.

23   The 'original' can be viewed at www.liverpoolmuseums.org.uk/picture-of-month/showLarge.asp?venue=7&id=299. The revised (Pears') version is at www.playle.com/pictures/WHIMZY871.jpg, accessed 17 June 2009.

24   Higonnet, *Pictures of Innocence*, pp. 51–71.

25   J. Berger, *Ways of Seeing*, Harmondsworth: Penguin Books, 1972, p. 134.

26   Ibid., p. 149.

27   Quoted from C. Hamilton, 'You don't have to be Humbert Humbert to See Child Sexualisation', *Crikey*, 5 June 2009.

28   C. Lumby, 'Art, Not Porn', *Age*, 25 May 2008.

29   A. Adler, 'The Perverse Law of Child Pornography', *Columbia Law Review* 101(2), March 2001, pp. 209–73; C. Kleinhans, 'Virtual Child Porn: The Law and the Semiotics of the Image', *Journal of Visual Culture*, 1, 2004, pp. 17–34; Edge and Baylis, 'Photographing Children'.

30   The image can be viewed at www.nationalgallery.org.uk/cgi-bin/WebObjects.dll/CollectionPublisher.woa/wa/work?workNumber=ng1314, accessed 19 June 2009.

31   See http://laloli.files.wordpress.com/2008/08/holbein_ambassadors_anamorphosis.jpg, accessed 19 June 2009.

32    J. Lacan, *The Four Fundamental Concepts of Psychoanalysis: The Seminar of Jacques Lacan, Book XI*, Jacques-Alain Miller (ed.), trans. Alan Sheridan, New York: W. W. Norton, 1998, pp. 79–90.

33    See R. D. Mohr, 'The Pedophilia of Everyday Life', *The Guide: Gay Travel, Entertainment, Politics & Sex*, Boston: Fidelity Publishing, January 1999, accessed at http://archive.guidemag.com/magcontent/invokemagcontent.cfm?ID=e6b2cf69-031d-11d4-ad990050da7e046b, 3 August 2010.

34    A. Geczy, 'Humbert or Humbug?', *Art Monthly Australia*, 211, July 2008, p. 11.

# Bibliography

Adler, Amy 2001, 'The Perverse Law of Child Pornography', *Columbia Law Review*, 101(2), March, pp. 209–73.

Agamben, Giorgio 2007, *Profanations*, trans. Jeff Fort, Brooklyn: Zone Books.

Althusser, Louis 1971, 'Ideology and Ideological State Apparatuses', in *Lenin and Philosophy and Other Essays*, trans. Ben Brewster, London: New Left Books, pp. 123–73.

Arendt, Hannah 1998, *The Human Condition*, Chicago: University of Chicago Press.

Ariès, Philippe 1973, *Centuries of Childhood*, Ringwood: Penguin Books.

Austin, J. L. 1962, *How To Do Things With Words*, Oxford: Clarendon Press.

Bakhtin, M. M. 1984 (1965), *Rabelais and His World*, trans. H. Iswolsky, Bloomington: Indiana University Press.

Barthes, Roland 1982, *Mythologies*, trans. Annette Lavers, London: Granada.

Bashford, Alison 2004, *Imperial Hygiene: A Critical History of Colonialism, Nationalism and Public Health*, New York: Palgrave Macmillan.

Bates, Daisy 1938, *The Passing of the Aborigines: A Lifetime Spent Among The Natives Of Australia*, London: Murray.

Benjamin, Walter 1968, 'The Work of Art in the Age of Mechanical Reproduction', in Hannah Arendt (ed.), *Illuminations*, trans. Harry Zohn, New York: Schocken Books, pp. 217–51.

Berger, John 1972, *Ways of Seeing*, Harmondsworth: Penguin Books.

—— 1980, 'Understanding a Photograph', in Alan Trachtenberg (ed.), *Classic Essays on Photography*, New Haven: Leete's Island Books, pp. 291–4.

Bion, Wilfred R. (ed.) 1967, *Second Thoughts: Selected Papers on Psycho-Analysis*, London: Karnac Books.

Bottigheimer, Ruth 1994, 'The Child-Reader of Children's Bibles, 1656–1753', in E. Goodenough, M. A. Heberle and N. Sokoloff (eds), *Infant Tongues: The Voice of the Child in Literature*, Detroit: Wayne State University Press.

Bourdieu, Pierre 1984, *Distinction: A Social Critique of the Judgement of Taste*, trans. Richard Nice, Cambridge, MA: Harvard University Press.

Burke, Anthony 2008, *In Fear of Security: Australia's Invasion Anxiety*, Melbourne and Cambridge: Cambridge University Press.

Castoriadis, Cornelius 1987, *The Imaginary Institution of Society*, trans. Kathleen Blamey, Cambridge: Polity Press.

—— 2007, *Figures of the Thinkable*, trans. Helen Arnold, Stanford: Stanford University Press.

Cline, Foster W. & Fay, Jim 1990, *Parenting with Love and Logic: Teaching Children Responsibility*, Colorado Springs: Pinon Press.

Connell, R. W., Ashenden, D. J., Kessler, S. & Dowsett, G. W. 1982, *Making the Difference: Schools, Families and Social Division*, Sydney: Allen & Unwin.

Cooper, Dennis 2009, 'Bill Henson: Ambiguous Spaces of Adolescence', *Pavement Magazine* 3, accessed at www.pavementmagazine.com/billhenson.html, 19 October 2009.

Devetak, Richard 2004, 'In Fear of Refugees: The Politics of Border Protection in Australia', *International Journal of Human Rights*, 8(1), Spring, pp. 101–9.

Devine, Miranda 2008, 'Moral Backlash Over Sexing Up of Our Children, *Sydney Morning Herald*, 22 May.

Doan, Alesha E. & Williams, Jean Calterone 2008, *The Politics of Virginity: Abstinence in Sex Education*, Westport: Praeger.

Douglas, Mary 2002, *Purity and Danger: An Analysis of the Concepts of Pollution and Taboo*, London and New York: Routledge Classics.

Djuric, Bonney 2008, *14 Years of Hell: An Anthology of the Hay Girls Institution 1961–1974*, Hay: Women About Hay.

Edge, Sarah & Baylis, Gail 2004, 'Photographing Children: The Works of Tierney Gearon and Sally Mann', *Visual Culture in Britain*, 5(1), Summer, pp. 75–90.

Foot, Matt 2005, 'A triumph of hearsay and hysteria', *Guardian*, 5 April.

Foucault, Michel 1979, *Discipline and Punish: The Birth of the Prison*, trans. Alan Sheridan, New York: Vintage.

—— 1990, *The History of Sexuality: Volume I: An Introduction*, trans. Robert Hurley, Ringwood: Penguin Books.

Freud, Sigmund 1977, 'Three Essays on the Theory of Sexuality', in Angela Richards (ed.), *On Sexuality*, The Penguin Freud Library, vol. 7, trans. James Strachey, Harmondsworth: Penguin Books.

—— 1960, *Totem and Taboo*, trans. James Strachey, London: Routledge and Kegan Paul.

Frost, Nick & Stein, Mike 1989, *The Politics of Child Welfare: Inequality, Power and Change*, New York and London: Harvester Wheatsheaf.

Gale, Julie 2008, 'The Sexualisation of Children', *Unleashed*, ABC *Online*, 3 March, accessed at www.abc.net.au/unleashed/stories/ s2175450.htm, 20 February 2009.

Gatens, Moira 1996, *Imaginary Bodies: Ethics, Power and Corporeality*, London and New York: Routledge.

Geczy, Adam 2008, 'Humbert or Humbug?', *Art Monthly Australia*, 211, July, pp. 9–13.

Guest, Ross 2007, 'The Baby Bonus: A Dubious Policy Initiative', *Policy*, 23(1), pp. 11–16.

Hage, Ghassan 1998, *White Nation: Fantasies of White Supremacy in a Multicultural Society*, Sydney: Pluto Press.

—— 2003, *Against Paranoid Nationalism: Searching for Hope in a Shrinking Society*, Sydney: Pluto Press.

Hamilton, Clive 2009, 'You Don't Have to be Humbert Humbert to See Child Sexualisation', *Crikey*, 5 June, accessed at https://www.crikey. com.au/2009/06/05/hamilton-you-dont-have-to-be-humbert- humbert-to-see-s-xualisation-of-kids/, 19 June.

Hewitt, David 2007, 'Bovvered? A Legal Perspective on the ASBO', *Journal of Forensic and Legal Medicine*, 14, pp. 355–63.

Higonnet, Anne 1998, *Pictures of Innocence: The History and Crisis of the Ideal Childhood*, London: Thames and Hudson.

Hobbes, Thomas 1968 (1651), *Leviathan*, C. B. Macpherson (ed.), Ringwood: Penguin Books.

Howard, John 2007, 'To Stabilise and Protect', address to the Sydney Institute, 25 June, accessed at www.abc.net.au/news/opinion/ speeches/files/20070625_howard.pdf, 23 February 2009.

Jackson, Stevi 1982, 'Understanding Everyday Experience', *Childhood and Sexuality*, Laurie Taylor (ed.) in Oxford: Basil Blackwell.

Kidd, Rosalind 2007, *Hard Labour, Stolen Wages: National Report on Stolen Wages*, Sydney: Australians for Native Title and Reconciliation.

Kincaid, James 1998, *Erotic Innocence: The Culture of Child Molesting*, Durham and London: Duke University Press.

Kipling, Rudyard 2000 (1899), 'The White Man's Burden: A Poem', in *McClure's Magazine*, 12.

Kleinhans, Chuck 2004, 'Virtual Child Porn: The Law and the Semiotics of the Image', *Journal of Visual Culture*, 3(1), pp. 17–34.

Lacan, Jacques 1998, *The Four Fundamental Concepts of Psychoanalysis: The Seminar of Jacques Lacan, Book XI*, Jacques-Alain Miller (ed.), trans. Alan Sheridan, New York: W. W. Norton.

Levander, Caroline F. 2006, *Cradle of Liberty: Race, the Child, and National Belonging from Thomas Jefferson to W.E.B. Du Bois*, Durham and London: Duke University Press.

Locke, John 1947 (1693), 'The Second Treatise of Civil Government', in Thomas I. Cook (ed.), *Two Treatises of Government*, New York: Hafner.

—— 1904–14, *Some Thoughts Concerning Education*, Vol. XXXVIII, part 1, The Harvard Classics, New York: P. F. Collier and Son; see also Bartelby.com 2001, www.bartelby.com/37/1/.

Lumby, Catherine 2008, 'Art, Not Porn', *Age*, 25 May, accessed at www.theage.com.au/news/opinion/art-not-porn/2008/05/24/ 1211183187056.html, 18 June 2009.

—— & Albury, Kath 2010, 'Too much? Too young? The sexualisation of children debate in Australia', *Media International Australia*, special issue: 'Children, Young People, Sexuality and the Media', 135, May, pp. 141–52.

MacNeill, Kate 2010, 'When Subject Becomes Object: Nakedness, art and the public sphere', *Media International Australia*, special issue: 'Children, Young People, Sexuality and the Media', 135, May, pp. 82–93.

Maddison, Sarah 2009, *Black Politics: Inside the Complexity of Aboriginal Political Culture*, Sydney: Allen & Unwin.

Manning, A. E. 1958, *The Bodgie: A Study in Psychological Abnormality*, Sydney: Angus & Robertson.

Marr, David 2008, *The Henson Case*, Melbourne: Text Publishing.

—— & Wilkinson, Marian 2004, *Dark Victory: How a Government Lied Its Way to Political Triumph*, Sydney: Allen & Unwin.

Marx, Karl 1859, *Critique of Political Economy*, trans. S. W. Ryazanskaya, accessed at www.marxists.org/archive/marx/works/1859/ critique-pol-economy/, 18 February 2009.

McKee, Alan 2010, 'Everything is Child Abuse', *Media International Australia*, special issue: 'Children, Young People, Sexuality and the Media', 135, May, pp. 131–40.

Mill, J. S. 1989, *On Liberty and Other Writings*, Stefan Collini (ed.), Cambridge: Cambridge University Press.

Mitchell, Don 1995, 'The End of Public Space? People's Park, Definitions of the Public, and Democracy', *Annals of the Association of American Geographers*, 85(1), pp. 108–33.

Mohr, Richard D. 1999, 'The Pedophilia of Everyday Life', in *The Guide: Gay Travel, Entertainment, Politics & Sex*, January, Boston: Fidelity Publishing, accessed at www.guidemag.com/magcontent/ invokemagcontent.cfm?ID=E6B2CF69–031D–11D4-

AD990050DA7E046B&method=GuideFullDisplay, 30 January 2009.

New South Wales Government Submission to the National Inquiry into the Separation of Aboriginal and Torres Strait Islander Children from Their Families, 1998, *Securing the Truth*, accessed at www.daa. nsw.gov.au/publications/securing_the_truth.pdf, 1 February 2008.

Nicolacopoulos, Toula & Vassilacopoulos, George 2008, 'Street Rivals: Jaywalking and the Invention of the Motor Age Street', *Technology and Culture*, 48, April, pp. 331–59.

————— 2004, 'Racism, Foreigner Communities and the Onto-pathology of White Australian Subjectivity', in Aileen Moreton-Robinson (ed.), *Whitening Race*, Canberra: Aboriginal Studies Press, pp. 32–47.

Norton, Peter D. 2007, *Fighting Traffic: The Dawn of the Motor Age in the American City*, Cambridge, MA: The MIT Press.

Patton, George C. et al. 2009, 'Global Patterns of Mortality in Young People: A Systematic Analysis of Population Health Data', *Lancet*, 374, 12 September, pp. 881–92.

Pierce, Peter 1999, *The Country of Lost Children: An Australian Anxiety*, Melbourne: Cambridge University Press.

Pilkington, Doris 1996, *Follow the Rabbit-Proof Fence*, St Lucia: University of Queensland Press.

Quart, Alissa 2003, *Branded: The Buying and Selling of Teenagers*, Cambridge, MA: Perseus Publishing.

————— 2006, *Hothouse Kids: The Dilemma of the Gifted Child*, New York: Penguin Books.

Qvortrup, Jens 1995, 'From Useful to Useful: The Historical Continuity of Children's Constructive Participation', *Sociological Studies of Children*, 7, pp. 49–76.

Rawls, John 1971, *A Theory of Justice*, Cambridge, MA: Belknap Press of Harvard University Press.

Riley, Denise 1983, *War In The Nursery: Theories of the Child and the Mother*, London: Virago Press.

Rose, Jacqueline 1984, *The Case of Peter Pan or The Impossibility of Children's Fiction*, London: Macmillan.

Rose, Nikolas 1989, *Governing the Soul: The Shaping of The Private Self*, London and New York: Routledge.

Rousseau, Jean-Jacques 1974, *Émile*, trans. Barbara Foxley, London and Melbourne: Everyman's Library.

Rush, Emma & La Nauze, Andrea 2006, 'Corporate Paedophilia: Sexualisation of Children in Australia', discussion paper no. 90, October, The Australia Institute, accessed at https://www.tai.org.au/ file.php?file=DP90.pdf, 23 January 2009.

———— 2006, 'Letting Children Be Children: Stopping the Sexualisation of Children in Australia', discussion paper no. 93, December, The Australia Institute, accessed at https://www.tai.org.au/file.php?file=DP93.pdf, 23 January 2009.

Sartre, Jean-Paul 2003, *Being and Nothingness: An Essay on Phenomenological Ontology*, trans. Hazel E. Barnes, London and New York: Routledge.

Senate Standing Committee on Environment, Communications and the Arts 2008, *Sexualisation of Children in the Contemporary Media*, Canberra: Senate Printing Unit.

Sibley, David 1995, *Geographies of Exclusion*, London and New York: Routledge.

Sidhu, D. 2005, 'Nocturne: The Photographs of Bill Henson', *Ego Magazine*, August, accessed at www.egothemag.com/archives/2005/08/bill_henson.htm, 20 May 2009.

Stanley, Lawrence A. 1991, ' "Perversion": Censoring Images of Nude Children', *Art Journal* 50(4), *Censorship II*, Winter, pp. 20–7.

Stavrakakis, Yannis 2007, *The Lacanian Left: Psychoanalysis, Theory, Politics*, Edinburgh: Edinburgh University Press.

Steward, James Christen 1995, *The New Child: British Art and the Origins of Modern Childhood, 1730–1830*, Seattle: University Art Museum and University of Washington Press.

Stone, Deborah 1997, *Policy Paradox: The Art of Political Decision Making*, London and New York: W. W. Norton.

Stone, Gregory P. 1965, 'The Play of Little Children', *Quest*, 4(1), pp. 23–31.

Stratton, J. 1984, 'Bodgies and Widgies – Youth Cultures in the 1950s', *Journal of Australian Studies* 8(15), pp. 10–24.

Stringer, Rebecca 2007, 'A Nightmare of the Neocolonial Kind: Politics of Suffering in Howard's Northern Territory Intervention', *borderlands e-journal*, 6(2), accessed at www.borderlands.net.au/vol6no2_2007/stringer_intervention.htm, 8 December 2009.

Taylor, Charles 2004, *Modern Social Imaginaries*, Durham: Duke University Press.

Turmel, André 2008, *The Historical Sociology of Childhood: Developing Thinking, Categorization and Graphic Visualization*, Cambridge: Cambridge University Press.

Valentine, Gill 2004, *Public Space and the Culture of Childhood*, Aldershot: Ashgate.

valentine, kylie 2008, 'Innocence defiled, again? The art of Bill Henson and the welfare of children', *Australian Review of Public Affairs*, June, accessed at www.australianreview.net/digest/2008/06/valentine.html, 21 May 2009.

Veblen, Thorstein 2007, *The Theory of the Leisure Class*, Oxford and New York: Oxford University Press.

White, Richard 1981, *Inventing Australia: Images and Identity 1688–1980*, Sydney: Allen & Unwin.

Wild, Rex & Anderson, Patricia 2007, *Ampe Akelyernemane Meke Mekarle (Little Children Are Sacred)*, Report of the Northern Territory Board of Inquiry into the Protection of Aboriginal Children from Sexual Abuse, accessed at www.inquirysaac.nt.gov.au/pdf/bipacsa_final_report.pdf, 8 December 2009.

Wilson, Ronald & Dodson, Mick 1997, *Bringing Them Home: Report of the National Inquiry into the Separation of Aboriginal and Torres Strait Islander Children from Their Families*, Sydney: Human Rights and Equal Opportunity Commission.

Young Media Australia, 'Classifications – films, videos, DVDs', www.youngmedia.org.au/codes/classifications_films.htm.

Zelizer, Viviana A. 1985, *Pricing the Priceless Child: The Changing Social Value of Children*, New York: Basic Books.

# Index

## Australian Encounters series

Cambridge University Press Australia, in partnership with the National Centre for Australian Studies at Monash University, presents Australian Encounters. Combining original scholarly research and elegant, accessible prose, this series engages with important Australian issues that span current society, politics, culture, economics and historical debates. It brings new thinking and fresh perspectives to these issues that are so vital to Australian society.

## Series Editor

Dr Tony Moore is Lecturer in Media and Communications and Director of the National Centre for Australian Studies, Monash University.

## Forthcoming titles in the Australian Encounters series

### Curtin's Empire

**James Curran**

Senior Lecturer in History at the University of Sydney argues for a revision of the popular myth of wartime Prime Minister John Curtin as an opponent of the British Empire.